braveing the way

Laurel C. Fox

braveing the way

Written by Laurel C. Fox

Back cover author photo by
Peggy Wilkie Photography

Published by
Laurel Carini Fox
Basalt, Colorado

ISBN: 979-8-9904981-9-8, Paperback
ISBN: 979-8-9904981-8-1, Hardcover
Library of Congress Control Number: 2024911338

Light of the Moon, Inc.
Empowering independent authors since 2009
Book Design/Production/Consulting
Carbondale, Colorado • www.lightofthemooninc.com

This book is dedicated to every parent and person who has been (or will be) a badass advocate.

I see you.

Foreword

In my two decades of medical practice, spanning from the bustling corridors of an inner-city hospital in Denver, Colorado, to the harrowing scenes of an emergency room in the aftermath of the Columbine mass shooting, I have borne witness to the unfathomable trauma that families endure in the blink of an eye. Yet amidst these tragedies, I have also witnessed the remarkable resilience of the human spirit and the innate healing intelligence of the heart to create a future of health, acceptance, and well-being.

In *braveing the way*, Laurel embarks on a profound journey, courageously baring her soul as a mother who received the dreaded phone call every parent fears. Throughout her career, Laurel has lent her voice to countless tales as a professional voice-over actor. But fate, it seems, had reserved a different role for her—one that required no script and no rehearsed lines.

braveing the way is her own story, a poignant chronicle of a parent and her daughter, Taylor, whose lives were irrevocably altered by a tragic accident and the stark reality of traumatic brain injury.

Each year in the United States, traumatic brain injuries afflict 2.8 million individuals, with eight hundred thousand of these cases occurring in teenagers between the ages of fifteen and nineteen. The spectrum of these injuries is vast, their repercussions often bearing tragic, long-term consequences. Navigating the arduous road to recovery demands a myriad of resources, from the initial throes of acute care in hospitals and ICUs to the ongoing support provided by a network of medical professionals, therapists, and caregivers.

The challenges faced by those grappling with traumatic brain injuries, alongside their families and caregivers, are immense, underscoring the vital importance of unwavering support from friends, family, and communities alike.

In *braveing the way*, Laurel unveils, through the lens of a parent, the anguish, grief, and overwhelming sense of loss that accompany the tumultuous journey of traumatic brain injury. With unwavering candor, she invites us into her world, allowing us to bear witness to the triumphs and tribulations, the highs and lows, and the profound bond shared between a parent and child—a bond that transcends both adversity and the confines of medical science.

Through her heartfelt narrative, Laurel bravely portrays the internal struggles of a parent, from the initial shock of the accident to the grueling days spent in the ICU, and the ensuing months of recovery. In doing so, she reveals not only the marvels of modern medicine but also the most potent healing force of all: the boundless capacity for love that resides within us all.

Within these pages, Laurel illuminates the serendipitous twists of fate that remind us of the universal allure of healing through sacrifice, forgiveness, and above all, love. Her tales of chance encounters and unforeseen allies serve as poignant reminders that, even in our darkest hours, there exists a beacon of hope, guiding us toward the path of healing and renewal.

braveing the way is more than just a story; it is a testament to the enduring strength of the human heart and a reminder that, even in our darkest moments, love has the power to illuminate the path forward. As you embark on this journey alongside Laurel and her daughter, may her words serve as both solace and inspiration, guiding you through the depths of despair toward the light of hope beyond.

Robert McDermott, MD
Founder,
Healing Intelligence Network

Healing
Intelligence
Network LLC

CONTENTS

Introduction

I never thought I would be so compelled to tell you my story; yet here I sit almost ten years to the day when my entire life turned upside down, choosing to share this with you. We all know that frightening and horrific things happen to good people every day. Sadly, I have lived through one of those days.

When it happens, some of us question it, some of us feel it deeply, some of us feel it so deeply we fall apart, and some of us feel it to our core, not knowing how to handle it. Each chosen one is forced to find their own way through it, however they are equipped to do so.

When something horrible happens to you or someone close to you, you can never prepare yourself for what the horrible might look like, what you will feel, or what you will have to do. You can attempt to prepare yourself for what lies ahead, but life isn't set up that way. I wound up surprising myself with what I ultimately bore, tolerated, and accomplished. When I was in my moment of sheer terror I was sure of one thing: I could not turn the clock back and get a do-over of 'that day.' I had to take what was happening and use everything inside me to catapult forward.

To me at that moment, there was no option other than to deal with what was happening, make it part of my life, and fight like hell. I knew I had to dig deep and find some serious strength. I also knew I had to stay hopeful in order to show up and be who I needed to be for my daughter. I had to accept the now, I had to be willing to forgive, and above all...I had to be brave. I just didn't know how.

I now have hindsight. I'll have it always, and I'll never, ever forget that I have it. I am constantly being reminded of the perspective I now have and because of that, I truly believe that without the bad we can't fully grasp and appreciate the good stuff. I'm not saying people can't feel the fullness of gratitude unless something bad happens to them. I'm saying that when you survive something and dig deep into yourself, your own perspective changes. I learned that when you are willing to expose the deepest parts of yourself, unexpected, beautiful things can happen and it can be soul changing—but only if you let it.

Growing up I had parents who were really happy; my mom especially had a cup that was always full. I was taught to look at the bright side of things when something horrible happens and find that silver lining. Or how about the famous everything happens for a reason line? Nope. Not in this story of mine. My beliefs have been put to the ultimate test and I can only tell you what I learned. I learned how to accept every little and big gift that was given to me. I also learned to attach that acceptance to everything that was happening. Not for my daughter, but for me.

I learned that life and what happens to each of us is something we cannot control. I also learned that the only thing that matters is being present in the moments we have, because guess what? It can change in a split second. I was forced to see the beauty in a dreadful situation, and it was the most painful thing I have ever done.

This is a story about a horrible thing that happened one day.

This is a story about what traumatic brain injury can do to a family, how difficult it is to be a survivor, and what recovery looks like.

This is also a story about love, of never giving up, and why human kindness is immeasurable.

It is a story of constant resilience.

It's about a community of people coming together with positive strength and encouragement, and how that can empower us.

Mostly it's a story about finding courage and how that was sparked by my fierce love for my kids.

In one of the darkest moments of my life, I wanted someone to hand me a book of instructions on what to do. A step-by-step manual, a guide, or anything of the sort. Turns out that type of book doesn't exist when the rug is literally pulled out from underneath you. I hope my story can help someone who needs a manual when they feel paralyzed in fear; or if someone feels like the trauma is bigger than they are and they can't possibly find the fight to get through it. I'm here to tell you that I *never* thought I could be as brave or as strong as I showed up to be.

Horrific things happen to people every day on this planet of ours. I can only hope that reading my story, and understanding my journey through my daughter's own separate journey, might help you find acceptance and bravery in something difficult. I didn't ask "Why me?" or "Why my daughter?" but I did spend a lot of time pondering the fact that we were the chosen ones.

The reason this happened? I might never know the reason. However, believing in some kind of meaning coming out of this became my everything. From the moment my entire world was demolished, I never stopped searching for the purpose in the horror. Honestly, I'm still searching. Something has happened to each of us.

Hello, my name is Laurel, and this is what happened to me...

part
one

CHAPTER 1

My New Job

It was around 4 am Thursday, June 5th, 2014, and my four-teen-year-old daughter, Taylor, was lying in a hospital bed. Most of the space in the room was taken up by the breathing machine, monitors, IVs, and all the other things that were functioning for her body because her brain couldn't. Her face looked swollen, and she was wearing a neck brace to hold her head steady. The neck brace was labeled ASPEN across the bottom, which distracted me for a split second. Interesting...since that's where I grew up. Why is that name on a neck brace?

Focusing back, I noticed several tubes covering her face and body. I could identify the one breathing for her, the one feeding her, and the one that was monitoring her brain activity. She was wearing giant boots on her feet up to her knees that were deflating and expanding to keep her circulation moving. She was bruised and scraped up, but I noticed she still had her eye makeup on from the day before. She looked like she was in a peaceful sleep. It was a strange sight for me.

I had spent the night on the bench next to her bed, trying to sleep, but for the most part that didn't happen. There was a lot of nurse and doctor activity every hour, so it was not quiet. They had to rotate her body to reduce the risk of bedsores, watch her brain swelling, check her vital signs, and watch all the other monitors hooked up to her.

Waking up that morning in the ICU after small fragments

of sleep, I saw Julie, her nighttime nurse, sitting at the desk outside Taylor's room. I took a deep breath as I sat crossed-legged on the bench next to Taylor. I realized we were by ourselves, and then it hit me. I knew in that second that I was ultimately alone in this. I knew that I had family and friends waiting to help in any way they could, but I knew this was going to be my new job. I would have to leave my job that pays me and dig into this one.

As I stared at Taylor in the dimly lit room, I was sure of two things. First, my life as I knew it was over, and second, I was not leaving this child's side. I could hear the sound of the ventilator breathing for Taylor. It was the only sound in the room, and the more I heard it, the calmer I felt. It was keeping Taylor alive, and it was doing something to me. The metronomic sound was almost hypnotizing, and I felt calm. Scary calm. Something I hadn't felt since getting that phone call. That's when it happened. That moment is still difficult for me to explain or put into words. A mixture of emotions engulfed my body. Anger, sadness, fear, anxiety, discomfort, loneliness, and fury. Is it really Taylor in that bed? Yes, yes it is.

With that, I also felt strength, excitement, happiness, and powerful energy run through me. At the risk of sounding a little *woo woo*, it felt like my body was being pushed toward Taylor in her bed. I started to cry when everything my eyes were seeing hit me like a punch, but I never lost sight of her. My thought as I stared through tears at my girl, *if she can do this, well then dammit so can I.*

I was going to be the one to get Taylor the best chance at a recovery. No one else could. My children have a wonderful father, Mike, but we had been divorced for five years. I had no boyfriend at the time. I had a job that I knew I couldn't go back to, but I knew I needed to keep my house, my car, and my health insurance. Nothing else mattered at that point except for Taylor and Emma. I knew I had to find the strength to move forward. I also knew I had to stay connected to the thought of making it to the other side by staying positive and hopeful. I would have to be Taylor's voice, which in turn would make me her advocate. I would be her main warrior with an entire army of doctors, nurses, school community, family, and friends beside us. I was determined to bring her back, and I would leave no stone unturned. It was crystal clear to me that Taylor and this entire shit show was now my job because I am her mom.

. . .

I spent the first two nights and days next to Taylor in that hospital room. I left her only to go sit in a room outside the ICU down the hall and through the big locked doors. It was a waiting room where I could see some family or friends, update them, sometimes have a good laugh or cry, and then go back to Taylor's bedside.

Kim, our day nurse, that second morning said, "Laurel, take this time and go home for a bit. This is the easy part right now because you have us taking care of her."

Boy, was she right about that! I went home to shower, spend some time with Emma, and get a good night's sleep in my own bed. I walked into our house and right away sensed how different it felt, almost eerie. I kept saying to myself, out loud, I have to get back to the hospital. I busied myself the best I could. Showered, packed a hospital bag, cleaned up, and dealt with Emma's dead fish while I waited for her to arrive home from being with her dad. Really? The fish too? Poor kid. Her dad dropped her off and I immediately grabbed onto her.

"Ouch, Mommy, you're hurting me!" Those were her exact words to me.

I didn't want to let her go, but I also knew that at some

point I had to tell Emma exactly what we were dealing with at the hospital, and also that Puddles, her fish, had kicked the bucket.

It crossed my mind that if I was ever going to turn to alcohol for some comfort, it would have started right then and there. I felt unnerved and anxious, especially as I prepared to tell Emma what was happening. When the conversation with Emma began, it was casual. She was unrattled, almost stoic, and I didn't want to ruin that for her. I gave her some time to take it in and then asked, "Do you want to ask me any questions about Taylor?"

"Kind of, but not really. No. Wanna play cards, Mommy?"

I knew this part wasn't going to be easy. I told her things slowly and carefully as we played a game of gin rummy, and the part that made her jump up was the news of Puddles. She ran over to his SpongeBob decked-out fish bowl, and I assured her as we both peered inside the tank, we would get her another betta fish as soon as things settled a little.

It was nice to sit and have Emma to myself for a bit, and I think it was also good for Emma to have some time with me. She knew I had been at the hospital and I looked okay, so everything must be okay. Right? Right. (No, but that was how her eleven-year-old self processed it.)

I tried to not dwell on the subject of Taylor and made the focus more about Emma's step-up day coming soon. When you're in sixth grade, it's a big deal when you graduate from the lower school. Those sixth graders go through days of rituals when they move onto the secondary campus to start seventh grade. Taylor was supposed to start ninth grade in September, and Emma was to be the little sister on campus as a brand new 'sevy,' as they called them. I wanted to throw up when I thought of it.

Emma was alone in her room when I went in to put some clothes away. I slowly wandered into Taylor's room to do the

10

same. It felt so different. We were here, and she wasn't. What was I doing folding her clothes? I realized I didn't know if she'd be back to wearing those clothes again. I didn't know if she would be back in that house, or when that would be, and that she could be in a wheelchair! Holy hell. I fell to my knees in Taylor's room, gripping her clean clothes, holding back a scream. I was crying and catching my breath when I saw Emma at the door.

"Are you okay Mommy?"

"I'm fine baby, I miss Taylor right now, but I'm okay," I said through tears. Emma started to cry but had to walk away.

The conversation with myself began. You're gonna get up and you're gonna start your new job, which is Taylor. Right here and right now. Part of that job includes Emma and making her feel safe, secure, and getting her through this next week as she graduates from sixth grade. Day by day, step by step, you will do this. Now up you go!

● ● ●

I used to complain about Taylor singing in the shower so loud that neighbors three houses down could hear her. I actually tested that out once by walking down the street. It was bothersome and frequently annoying if you were watching TV, or on a phone call, and Taylor was in the background at full volume with shower acoustics surrounding her. She had an extremely powerful voice, and she was known as a loud and long shower-taker. As I thought of her showering, it pained my heart to think how desperately I wanted her back in this house. I wanted to hear her singing at full volume and wasting as much water as she wanted. I wanted her here—and not where she was.

I was suddenly grateful for the simplest little things that Taylor brought to us. I wanted her on the couch hogging the

TV, I wanted her at the dinner table, and I wanted her arguing with Emma in the bathroom again. I missed the ordinary, everyday things that happened because Taylor was around. Now she wasn't.

●　●　●

My first goal would be to learn everything in order to be the best advocate I could for Taylor. The end goal would be to get her well enough to come home. What that looked like, I couldn't even imagine.

By day four in the hospital things began to get serious and occasionally overwhelming. Doctors and nursing staff met with Mike and/or myself every afternoon to talk about the past twenty-four hours, and to create a strategy to tackle the days ahead. Taylor was spiking fevers, getting infections, and her vitals were peaking and dipping. Her medical team expressed some concern, which led to a discussion about putting some strict rules in place. I was on board right away and made the decision that only her dad and I would be allowed in Taylor's space. If you were on the list of visitors in the lobby, then you were allowed into the waiting room outside the ICU. That waiting room wound up being my saving grace by always having some form of friends or family in it. It was comforting to know that someone could be twenty steps away if I needed a diversion from Taylor in a coma down the hall. That's when I knew my new job had officially started.

Welcome.

CHAPTER 2

'That Day'

Wednesday, June 4th, 2014.

At 6:45 in the morning, I was leaving for work and distinctly remember locking the back door. This was unusually early for me, since I normally took my daughters to school at 8 am. Taylor and Emma were inside the house getting ready and waiting for their dad to pick them up. He would drop Taylor off at her campus and then go on to work where Emma was in sixth grade. Their dad worked at their school, and the girls had gone there since kindergarten.

I still remember standing outside the closed backdoor of my house and staring at the silver lock as I went to put the key in. It was wet. This was June, a week before summer vacation for the girls, and mornings were gloomy here this time of year. I noticed tears of dew dripping down the lock, and I took a moment. I was suddenly overcome with a wish so strong I could barely turn the key. The thought was, *I want to be with my girls, I don't want to go to work today, and I want to be able to spend the summer with them.* I turned the key, walked to the car reluctantly, and drove to work.

I didn't really love what I was doing at the time, and I didn't really feel connected to it, but I was divorced and being a mom. Not working was not an option. I had decided a few weeks prior that I would stick with it for six months to a year while I explored other options if they came my way. I was a personal assistant for a lovely couple in Beverly Hills. I had been personal assisting for thirteen years, and had started working for them six months prior in December. They were great to work for, and I was slowly turning the household and staff into a well-managed machine. I have great systems to put in place for people who don't have a knack for organizing. It was working out well, though I was unfortunately feeling like I wasn't doing anything important. I certainly didn't feel like I was contributing to making the world a better place. I was helping them, and for right now, that had to be enough.

For some distraction on my drive to work, I blasted the song that had been on constant replay in the car with Taylor. One we liked to sing together and she had performed it at school five days prior in an arts festival. "Let It Go" by Idina Menzel, from the movie, *Frozen*. I was singing like a rock star in the car, which always made me feel better. I got through the morning and was excited for a first date that I had that evening. I had been talking to a guy I had met for a couple of weeks online, and we had planned to meet in person for the first time. Besides having a date at 7:00 that evening, I don't remember much about what happened during the day, until around 1:45 that afternoon.

I was talking to an insurance agent on the landline in the office when my cell phone rang. I didn't recognize the number and kept staring at the small screen as I tried to focus on the quotes the man was giving me. It was an 818 number, the same area code as everyone in the San Fernando Valley, but there was no name attached, and I couldn't think of who it might be. I noticed that the unknown number had left a message and then tried me a second time. I finished my call as quickly as I could to listen to the voicemail.

"Laurel, this is Damon from school...and um, Taylor was hit by a car and uh..."

I dropped the phone onto my desk and started screaming, "What the hell is happening?!" Gasping for air, I felt my body sinking into the floor. I felt heavy. Like I was in quicksand as I held onto the desk. The housekeeper came running into the office, and through scattered thoughts I said, "Mindy, my daughter was hit by a car at school, and I have to go."

I still felt heavy and had a hard time moving my legs. Mindy was clearly distraught as she helped me gather my things so I wouldn't forget anything. I told her to please call our boss and let her know. I frantically ran out of the office and told her I would be in touch.

I got in my car and tried to call Damon over and over. He wasn't answering. I started to drive and kept pushing Damon's number on my phone to redial him. I tried him six times before he finally answered.

Damon was one of Taylor's favorite teachers at school. Just a super cool dude, and he always had something clever to say to Taylor. They shared a special handshake that always made me smile.

I was frantic. "Damon, what is happening?"

On the other end of the phone Damon's voice, usually so jovial and vibrant, was unsure and shaky. "Laurel, Taylor was hit by a car, and they're putting her in the ambulance."

"Damon, stay with me, please. Don't hang this phone up. You have to find out where she's going. I'm in the car and I'll drive to where they're taking her. Tell me where to go, and please don't hang up on me."

"I won't. I'm going to hand the phone to Mitch."

Mitch was the principal at the time, and he knew Taylor well. I was pleading for information as my voice started to quiver.

"Mitch, I don't understand. She was at school, how did this happen? What is going on?! Please tell me what's happening!" I didn't ask him how Taylor was, or if she was bleeding or broken, unconscious or conscious, or even talking. I couldn't ask because deep inside I knew it was bad.

"I don't know, I don't know," he said. "I'm right next to the ambulance, and she's inside and they're working on her."

My heart completely sank. Crap. It's definitely bad. "Where is she going?" I asked. "Where are they taking her, and Mitch, please don't hang up this phone." I started to cry but knew I had to focus on the road. My goal was to get to her. I could hear Mitch talking to the ambulance driver, and in the background I could hear sirens and loud voices.

"Laurel, they're taking her to Northridge Hospital."

"Okay, thank you. I'm going there now."

I got on the freeway and realized that, though I was going in the right direction, I didn't know the specific location of the hospital. I called my friend Nancy. As soon as she answered, I immediately started crying. "Nance, I have no idea what happened, but there's been an accident at school and Taylor was hit by a car."

"What?" she gasped.

"I need you to tell me where to go because I'm driving to Northridge Hospital, I'm so freaked out, and I don't know where it is," I said through tears.

"Okay, hold on. Where are you?"

Nancy stayed on the phone with me until I exited the freeway. She told me where to go from there and said she was on her way to meet me there. My phone rang right away after that call. It was Mike. He didn't know that I was already on my way, and I had spoken to Damon. Mike's voice was trembling as he tried to speak.

"I know, I know." I cried.

Mike told me they were taking her to Northridge Hospital and that his brother, Dave, was in the ambulance with her. I told him I was already on my way, and I was close. I pushed the button on my steering wheel to hang up the call and could only think of Dave, a teacher on the campus, in that ambulance with Taylor. I started to take deep breaths to calm my nerves in order to stay focused. I knew I had to get there, keep my head on straight, and deal with this the best I could. If I couldn't do that, I knew I wouldn't make it there.

● ● ●

I followed the signs to the ER entrance and pulled in, looking for Taylor or the ambulance that brought her. Not seeing anything, I quickly parked my car and then made a conscious decision to walk and not run to the entrance door. I thought about what this could look like and began to prepare myself. I didn't like this scenario at all and started to feel sick to my stomach.

I pushed through the doors below the emergency entrance sign and immediately eyed the gentleman at the desk. I told him I was there for my daughter who was just brought in by an ambulance. He asked me for her name and then mine. I showed him my ID, and within two minutes the charge nurse came out of the door to get me. I was in complete shock and don't really remember what she said to me, but I do remember her being gracious and especially concerned about how I was doing. She walked me down the hallway twenty feet, and then I saw a vision that I still to this day, see often. Rounding the corner down the hallway came two police officers standing on each side of a doctor walking toward us. The three of them looked somber and eerily serious. That is when my knees buckled for the first time in my life, and I had to grab onto the wall. I felt like I couldn't move, so I stayed right where I was.

They approached me. I gasped as I put my hands together on top of my head. Dr. Kang introduced himself and then told me Taylor had been taken down for a CT scan. I wanted to see her, but I knew I couldn't. I would have to wait to ask the many questions I had for Dr. Kang. He assured me he would have more information after he received those results and would come find me as soon as he knew anything. He then asked Alicia, the charge nurse, to take me to a room where I could wait. I remember him apologizing for not knowing more, but I also recall that he was clearly concerned. I thanked him and followed Alicia into the room where Taylor's Uncle Dave was waiting. I could see he was crying and extremely upset. I started firing off questions to Dave while he hung his head in between his shoulders. He wasn't answering me at first, and it was hard for him to speak. He told me it was all awful; the scene was horrific, and he had seen the man driving the car. My ears perked up for a moment. Dave told me that man was going crazy, crying and trying to get to Taylor while police held him back. Through tears, Dave said he saw the driver freaking out about what had happened, screaming that he couldn't stop. He couldn't stop. I thought of him for a moment, wondering what he looked like, and then I snapped back to my reality of Taylor.

I started to get really scared. Oh my God, is Taylor going to die? No, Taylor is not going to die. Is she going to be okay? What does she look like? Her head, her body. Questions were racing through my mind. How bad was it? Was she bleeding? Could you see her face? Was she talking? That's when the priest entered the room, and I completely lost it. I started saying, "Oh my god, oh my god," and climbing the couch to get away from him. I had to get out of there and I did. I apologized to him and told him to not take it personally. I couldn't stay cooped up in that room. He was very kind, but I wasn't ready.

I went to find the exit door and as I pushed it open I saw fifty-some people that I knew had gathered. Some were waiting, some were talking to each other, some were crying, and most had reacted to me coming out of the door. I saw Nancy walk up, and I latched onto her. I said I didn't know anything yet and told some people that Taylor was in a CT scan and that we would hopefully know more soon. Mike finally got there, and we both went inside together while everyone else stayed where they were, willing to wait. After five minutes of standing in the hallway, I went back outside to get some air. I saw a lot of friends, relatives, and school staff gathering and comforting each other. Everyone looked extremely disheartened.

I glanced at a friend who was pointing to me as she spoke to a police officer. The officer approached me and introduced herself. She was a tall California Highway Patrol officer in a brown uniform. She asked me if we could step away for a moment while she asked me some questions regarding my daughter, Taylor.

"Yes, of course," I said. Oh my God, that is my daughter in there. Holy crap.

We stepped away to the side of the entrance doors, and I leaned against the brick building as I started feeling somewhat unstable. The officer proceeded to ask me questions. How much did Taylor weigh and how old was she? What time did Taylor wake up this morning? What did she eat for breakfast? What did she eat for lunch? As I slowly recalled the inventory of what I had packed in her lunch that morning, I started to feel nauseous. I excused myself from the officer and ran across the walkway to a trash can and threw up.

"Holy shit," was all I could think to say, and I started to sob as I squatted down next to the trash can. The officer was at my side and asked if I was okay, and if she could take me inside to get me some water or something. I assured her I was fine as I sat with my head between my legs and told her I needed a minute. She thanked me and said we were finished and if there was anything she could do, to please let her know.

"I know this is really difficult for you, Mom, so be sure and take care."

"Thank you," I said, as I began to tear up again.

I walked down an alleyway and called my mom in Colorado. As soon as she answered with her peppy little hello, I started to cry. "Oh, Mom..."

I couldn't say anything else since I was sobbing too hard.

"Laurel, what is it? I can't really understand you, honey."

I composed myself and told her what happened. I could hear her gasping for air and not really knowing what to say. My mom also felt like she was falling into the Earth. She was attached to both of my girls. It was horrible news to not only be sharing but to be hearing as well. I knew that.

I asked my mom to call my four sisters and anyone else she could think of. We needed everyone to send good thoughts Taylor's way. I told my mom to start calling on every guardian angel she knew, and send them to us. I somehow knew I needed a miracle at this point.

I said to her, through tears, "Oh, Mom, I don't know if I can do this by myself..."

She listened to me sob for a while, and after crying with me for a minute she said, "Laurel Ann, you are a strong woman and I know you can. You can do anything. I know you, and I know that love will support you through this. You can do this, honey." We both continued to cry.

Little did I know that those words from my precious mom would be the ones I reflect back on the most, even now. I told her I would speak to her soon when I knew more. We said goodbye, and I took a squat position and kept sobbing into my hands until I couldn't anymore. That was not an easy phone call to make.

As I walked back to the emergency entrance, I saw Mike waving at me to come inside. Taylor was back from her CT scan and we were going in to see her. The charge nurse asked if we were ready as we stood outside the double swinging doors to the room where Taylor was. We both nodded. I was just as ready to go in that room as I was to jump out of an airplane at thirty-thousand feet. Skydiving has never been of interest to me. I focused on Alicia's calm eyes as I inhaled to steady myself as we entered the cold room.

Taylor was lying on a bed, and the triage nurse was standing next to her with a chart in his hand. His name was Oscar, and I will never forget him. She was sleeping peacefully, but the tubes down her throat and all around her face disturbed me the most. I went up to her head and started stroking it and looking at every little piece of her I could see. Blood coming out of her ear, scrapes all over her face, mascara still on her eyelashes, and holy shit buckets, they had to cut all her clothes off. I couldn't really believe this was happening as I listened to the machines beeping in the background. Oscar explained that he would read through all of her injuries, and when he was finished he would answer any questions we might have.

"Does that sound okay?" he asked us. "Then when we're through here, we'll transfer her up to a room in the ICU on the third floor. Taylor will remain in critical condition and in an induced coma until doctors say otherwise."

Oscar handed me a list of her injuries so I could follow along as he explained them briefly.

Pedestrian versus automobile motor vehicle accident:

1) Traumatic brain injury with diffuse axonal injury
2) Traumatic encephalopathy
3) Occipital skull fracture extending into the base
4) Intraventricular hemorrhage
5) Subarachnoid hemorrhage
6) Subdural hemorrhage
7) Nondisplaced fracture of the third metatarsal bone on the left foot
8) Third cranial nerve palsy
9) Right inferior pubic rami fracture

10) Right-side sacral fracture

11) Right-side hemiplegia (paralysis)

The only two things that really stuck out to me were, traumatic brain injury and right-side paralysis? "Wait, paralysis?" Yes, paralysis. I sat in a chair next to Taylor and held her hand while Oscar finished reviewing her injuries with us. He showed us her right leg, which looked like an animal had chewed on it from the asphalt, and other various things on her body that would be a priority. Bruises, swelling, cuts, and scrapes everywhere. Mike had left the room, and I looked into Oscar's eyes as he was standing there holding the clipboard directly across from me at Taylor's chest. I didn't even have to say anything for him to say, "You know what, Mom...I've seen a lot worse in here, and she might be okay."

"I sure hope you're right Oscar...I sure hope you're right."

While tears fell I stood up and whispered in Taylor's ear. "Mama's here baby, and we're gonna get you better. I'm here and I got you."

I sat back down in the chair and put my head on her bed. All I could do was cry. I held on to her hand and thought to myself, *okay, brain injury.* It happened to someone I knew in high school, but I don't know how he's doing. Right-side paralysis, does that mean she won't walk again? I silently begged for that not to be true. I sat with her and took the moment to look at Taylor, feel her next to me, and send her good energy. Oscar had walked away, and I couldn't believe that it was us sitting there in that room. I stood up so I could walk around to her feet. I stood there and shut my eyes. I wanted it to not be real, and to not be happening to her. I started to cry and shake as my body fell onto her bed at her feet, the whole time thinking, *How the hell am I going to do this?* As I caught my breath and stood up, a calm feeling engulfed my body. At that point I wasn't sure if I was going to pass out or what was happening to me. I walked over to the chair to sit down and hung my head toward the floor in between my legs. Looking at the underside of the chair, I vowed to be strong for Taylor from the moment I sat back up.

I sat with Taylor for ten minutes or so until they asked me to see Alicia, the charge nurse. She had papers for me to sign before we were able to move Taylor upstairs. I went out the door of the triage room and saw five or six firemen standing against the opposite wall of the hallway next to Alicia. A few of them were still in their big yellow jackets and helmets, which immediately caught my eye. I paused next to them, and one by one they said how sorry they were. A few physically large men were noticeably emotional and quite shaken up. I hugged them and through tears thanked them for being there to help her. I knew they were her crew because they were extremely concerned about Taylor's condition, telling me they would be thinking of us. I thanked them profusely and wished I could have told them some good news, but I had none.

As I walked away from the paramedics and firemen I thought of them arriving there and what they had to witness in the aftermath. I couldn't imagine it. I know that I had received a phone call no parent wants to get, but those men and women had received the horrifying dispatch call and were the first ones to the scene. What they witnessed had to have been awful, and I had a deep amount of respect and empathy for them in that hallway. I know it was difficult for them because I saw it on each of their faces.

As I walked down the hospital corridor I felt grateful. Grateful for the doctors, nurses, and first responders who had helped Taylor. She would be in their thoughts. Feeling light-headed, I closed my eyes, crouched down to the ground, and whispered to myself, "Oh my God, please help me somehow muster the strength I need for this. Please."

. . .

I proceeded to walk outside to call Ryan, my date that I had been looking forward to that night. He answered, and I felt a tinge of pain in my stomach. When I hung up with him, I took a minute and leaned against a cement wall. I was entirely shocked at how kind he was. He offered to come to the hospital right then, to come the next day to bring me lunch, or whatever I needed. Ryan was compassionate and I really appreciated that, but a heavy thought came to mind: that no one was going to want to be a part of this. I never spoke to Ryan again.

CHAPTER 3

Here We Are

Taylor was hit by a car while she was walking across the street. It was a car that the driver couldn't stop while he was exiting a freeway off-ramp near her school. The kids were in the crosswalk at the bottom of the off-ramp, and the car went careening into them. Taylor and fifteen of her classmates were walking back to the gym after playing volleyball in the park adjacent to their school during physical education class. Three girls were hit. Two girls woke up on the concrete in the middle of the four-lane boulevard, lying in their own blood from injuries. One suffered a cruel leg and knee injury, and the other a badly torn up arm. Those two girls both remember 'that day,' and obviously suffer from the emotional trauma of it all.

Taylor suffered the worst injury by being catapulted fifty feet across all four lanes of traffic, landing on the left side of her head. First responders could tell right away that she had a brain injury. Blood was coming out of her ears, and her body was having a seizure. Taylor, in that moment, was going through a shift, fighting for her life.

I was also thrust into an unsettling shift, but I knew I had to make a conscious choice to be as present as possible. Starting then. No looking back. In those first hours at the hospital, I wanted to be able to talk to someone who had stood in my shoes. I wondered if that could ever happen.

I looked down at my feet which were starting to ache, and noticed my size-six Converse that I saw that morning at home as I tied them up. They were now standing with me in the hallway of a pediatric ICU. Across the hall from me was my daughter in a room with eight doctors and nurses fussing over her. I had my back pressed against the wall and I started to let gravity take over. I slid down the wall, until my butt hit the ground. I remember taking note that it felt good to let go until I felt that cold floor supporting me. I sat there against the wall with my knees folded up against my body, almost in a ball. I watched the staff carefully transition Taylor from one bed to another. I heard the doctor do a count to three while seven medical staff (all assigned to different positions around Taylor) lifted her effortlessly. They were each holding a section of the sheet, and it looked like she was floating across the room. I wondered how many times they had done that before to a fourteen-year-old girl who had been hit by a car.

I eavesdropped as the doctors and nurses who delivered her from the emergency room relayed information back and forth between each other and the ICU team. The ICU staff was listening intently and asking questions as they were taking over her care, reading charts, checking stats, etc. That was when I met Kim. Kim was the nurse in charge of Taylor during the day, and she would usually leave around 7:00 at night after she relayed all the details of the day to Julie, the night nurse. Little did I know that I would be spending a lot of time with these amazing nurses and that we would remain friends to this day.

There were a couple of hours of Kim's shift left, and she was taking time to explain some rules and ropes of the unit to me. Kim was watching a monitor over Taylor's head when she said, "You know you just won the lottery, right? Unfortunately, it's not the good lottery. And it's a long road, Mom, but I hope you can hang in there."

I sort of laughed while thinking, *What I would give to trade in* this *lottery ticket right now.* Wow. I'd truly give anything. Kim meant this didn't happen every day in her world, and it certainly doesn't happen often or to an innocent fourteen-year-old at school. The odds of this happening to us? The exact odds never crossed my mind. That's what the odds looked like to me. Never.

I quickly assured Kim that I would do all I could, and I would do anything that she asked of me to help Taylor or them. I would fight the fight to get her back, and although patience at the time wasn't my best quality, I would learn it. I had won the lottery no one wants to win. It all felt surreal.

I was unloading snacks and water that a friend had brought, attempting to get us comfortable in our twenty-five square foot room in the pediatric ICU of Northridge Hospital. From Taylor's CT scan and brain MRI, we had been told that anything could happen. Taylor had five substantial brain bleeds, and the goal was to watch all of them, monitor brain pressure, and then watch those bleeds some more. We had no idea what the damage looked like at this point with Taylor in a coma. Nor would we know anything regarding her recovery until some time passed. Dr. Kang and his team told us she might not walk again and she may never speak again. We knew nothing except that her road to recovery would be long and grueling.

"If she does either of those things again, who knows when that will happen or what that might look like? I'm really sorry I can't tell you much of anything right now," said Dr. Kang.

So many things were laid out as the worst-case scenario that I had to take a walk around the hospital. It was too much to soak in. Basically, the plan was to rest Taylor's brain and let time tell. They would keep her in an induced coma for as long as they thought necessary, and at the right time, they would start to wake her. The only thing I was sure of at that point was that she was in good hands.

I came back and started to settle into Taylor's room a

bit more by learning what machines were monitoring what, and which numbers were important to watch. Brain pressure, brain activity, oxygen levels, and the ventilator percentage would be my focus. Of course, moving her limbs as often as we could was important as well. I sat down on the bench next to Taylor's bed and slipped my Converse off. As my shoes fell to the ground making a loud thud, I remember thinking, *Here I am and this is where we are. Taylor and I, alone.* The revelation hit me that this is my daughter in the hospital bed next to me, and this is actually happening to us.

* * *

Two months ago, Taylor had turned fourteen years old; she was in the last week of eighth grade, and it was to be the last day of PE class before summer started. What are the odds of that? Oh yeah, that damn lottery again.

I was in an ICU for the first time in my life, and my daughter was now in critical condition on life support. She was in a life-threatening coma, and this morning had been a regular Wednesday. Here we are.

"In the unlikely event of an emergency
the oxygen masks will drop from above.
Make sure your mask is secure
before helping others."
airline safety demonstration

CHAPTER 4

The Journey Begins

From a deep place of thoughtfulness and hope, I made the decision to keep an online journal. I knew that I needed to share Taylor's daily progress in detail with people who wanted and deserved to know. There were many friends close to us and people who had heard that Taylor was in critical condition. Those people would be anxiously awaiting any news of change, progress, or anything at all.

I also knew being in this hospital bubble almost every day would make it difficult to communicate and spread the word to so many people. I couldn't possibly keep in contact with everyone via texts and phone calls. My phone was already blowing up and the communication part quickly became daunting.

The morning after 'that day,' the hospital asked me to make a statement to the press. A lot of them had been camped outside the hospital most of the night, which made me pause. I knew I couldn't go in front of a camera or talk about it yet, but when I saw the group of reporters and cameras outside, I knew a lot of people were genuinely concerned. Taylor was extremely beloved at her school, and the news was spreading fast through North Hollywood and five other private schools in the surrounding area. Parents, teachers, kids, and a whole community were rooting for her. I wrote a statement to the press, and that is where finding comfort in writing began for me.

We are deeply saddened by this horrific thing that has happened, and we obviously hope for a full recovery for our daughter. She is in critical condition at this time, and we ask that you please respect our privacy and continue to send good thoughts our way. We appreciate the outpouring of love and support from our friends, families, and everyone in our beautiful school community.

I instinctively felt and believed that if I reached out through a daily update, the love from so many people would make its way to Taylor and somehow help her. I held onto that thought and knew that I needed all the friends I could rally up to be in Taylor's corner.

The online journal named 'Taylor's Journey' would automatically send updates to people as they were posted, but they could also write to us if they felt so inclined. Throughout this journey there would be 30,000 people cheering Taylor on, sending messages from Scotland, and England. Even a holy thread from India came her way. The journal eventually became my daily comfort in countless isolated hospital days.

•   •   •

Taylor spent eight nights in the Northridge Hospital Trauma Pediatric Intensive Care Unit. On day nine, Dr. Kang decided to stop giving Taylor the coma-inducing medication, Propofol. Luckily, she had begun to breathe a little on her own twelve hours prior. This also meant that she wouldn't need to be intubated anymore, which was great news. I like to think this happened because I had whispered in her ear the night before.

"Taylor, girl, if you don't start to breathe on your own you'll need to get surgery for a tracheotomy in the front of your neck tomorrow. So please breathe, baby. Please, breathe."

Taylor started to breathe just enough on her own the next morning around 10:00, whether she heard me or not. This was the day that Dr. Kang felt confident that he was able to discharge her and send her on to the next hospital.

Something you should know. In the background of all of this chaos was the insurance company, which had many hospitals in the Los Angeles area calling Dr. Kang every day to check on Taylor's progress. They wanted to be in charge of her care and also wanted to admit her into their hospital as soon as possible. Kaiser Permanente was Taylor's health insurance, so I understood why they wanted to be making all of the decisions. I also knew that the Northridge trauma unit was one expensive place. When I heard of Kaiser trying to get her transferred to them, Dr. Kang and I had a discussion. I was feeling vulnerable and extremely sensitive to any change at that point. Dr. Kang was our constant and our everything for Taylor. He reassured me that he would not let a transfer happen one hour before it was time.

He was thoughtful and adamant in telling me, "they will wait if I need them to, and I won't let them take her one minute before I think she's ready." He then looked at me with that *I'm about to say something really difficult* look on his face. "Laurel, I think you should start to prepare, and look into having a wheelchair ramp put in your house. Both you and Mike. Think about making it accessible for her, and how Taylor may have to live at home in a different way from now on...I know this isn't easy to hear. I don't know when she might go home, but I want your family to be prepared, even for that worst case scenario."

I looked down at the floor and said, "I know," shaking my head and starting to well up with tears.

He looked me straight in the eye and continued "...I also hope I'm really wrong, and that you won't need any of that. One thing you should know is I love to be proven wrong."

That is when I hugged him for the first time but certainly not the last. I know Dr. Kang didn't want to see Taylor leave his unit quite yet. He had not only bonded with her, he was also deeply invested in her survival, her care, and her progress. Perhaps doctors have to keep a distance from their patients in some way for their own sanity. How difficult it must be to let a patient go after spending eight nights at the hospital away from your own family to be with them. Being completely immersed in her care, bonding with the family, and then nothing. As a doctor, you don't get to know how it turns out in the end. In most cases, you have to say goodbye, and then you're on to the next patient who takes that hospital room. I sensed an appreciation for him in that moment like no other.

Minutes before the ambulance got there for Taylor's transfer, she had opened both eyes for the first time on her own. Even though she had a panicked look in them, those eyes were open. Dr. Kang was speaking to her to possibly get her to respond. To perhaps look at him, squeeze his hand, or get some kind of eye contact. Nothing. When he opened her right eyelid to check for any signs, I noticed Taylor's right eyeball was extremely off-center and hugging the right side of her head. A small portion of it was showing and not budging at all with Dr. Kang's coaxing. That felt like a swift punch to my gut. He told me there was no response from her right pupil, which was concerning. Taylor was completely frozen on her right side, which we knew, but eye dilation functions with nerves. Even the right side of her face looked limp. I watched him put some last-minute notes into her chart as I thought about nerve damage. Oh no.

I started to play some music for my distraction while I gathered and packed the rest of our things from her room. I noticed that Taylor was hearing it and decided to turn on a song she loved from the TV show *Smash* and play it a little louder. Taylor's eyes lit up a bit and I could see that she was not only hearing the music, but I knew she recognized it when I saw her raise her left arm in the air. Dr. Kang saw this happen.

"Wow," he said, as he walked over to watch her more closely. Knowing that overstimulation was a factor, I only played the music for a minute, but it was truly amazing to see her actually respond to it like she did. It gave me hope in the moment, and it was an excellent goodbye for Dr. Kang.

Her ambulance transfer had arrived, and the paramedics who came to load her up stepped aside for Dr. Kang to say his goodbye to Taylor in the hallway. I was crying and thanking him for everything he had done. I really believed he had saved Taylor's life. From hour one he never left us, and I assured him I would stay in touch and update him on her progress.

Dr. Kang looked at me and said, "That sure would be great, and remember I like to be proven wrong."

"I know," I said, "And I really hope to do that someday. My eye is on that prize!" I said sassily, and he snickered.

That was a difficult goodbye, knowing I would have to stay open and trust many other doctors down the road (even though he was secretly my favorite).

Taylor slept through the entire ambulance ride and was transferred into the ICU at Kaiser Permanente Los Angeles. I was well aware they had been anxious to have Taylor under their care, so I was skeptical at first and already missing Dr. Kang. I was sure they wanted Taylor in their hospital mostly for financial reasons, but I wanted to stay positive and embrace the change for Taylor. Right away I learned the staff was kind, welcoming, and privy to her case. My main goal was to let them know how precious Taylor was and how lucky they were to have her. Apparently, Dr. Kang had already relayed that information and the woman who met me at the ambulance entrance assured me Taylor would be well taken care of. Taylor spent four nights in the Kaiser Permanente Los Angeles Pediatric Intensive Care Unit, and once she was finally transferred into the pediatric hospital wing on day thirteen, the real work began. For all of us.

Journal Entry Day 13
June 16th, 2014

I want you all to know that I read each one of your messages. There are moments in the day and night when I need to feel your arms wrapping around us, and I do.

Today Taylor was transferred from intensive care to the pediatrics unit. That meant a lot of visits from new doctors, surgeons, etc. Her surgery to get a more efficient feeding tube (a mic-key button) in her belly, was pushed until the end of the week. For now, she has a feeding tube in her nose that she will hopefully get used to. In a moment of wakefulness last night, Taylor latched onto the tube with her left hand. She didn't like it and tried like hell to yank it out, which caused an alarm. Other than that there is not much to report.

Taylor has suffered from a severe TBI (traumatic brain injury) and it's not an easy thing to understand. Hopefully, because she has youth on her side, her brain will rebuild itself. That's what we need to happen.

When you're told that we won't know anything for a long while, and we won't know what the recovery process looks like or how long that will take, if there even is one, it can feel frustrating, to say the least. It's a waiting game, it's a test of faith, and a true test of patience. Taylor needs a lot of time until we know more. Everyday I hope for the patience to get through this and the faith to hang on. Thank you all for helping us through this journey. And it looks like it will be a journey of one baby step at a time.

Love to all of you,
Laurel

part
two

CHAPTER 5

My Backstory

I was born in Brookfield, Wisconsin in 1970. My dad was a successful car dealer in Milwaukee, and I reflect on my childhood often as being absolutely wonderful. We lived in a luxurious house, and we had everything we needed, including a vacation home in little Snowmass Village, Colorado.

My parents divorced when I was nine years old, and my mom moved my four sisters and me to our vacation home in Snowmass Village. Sure, I missed my dad, but when you're nine you don't get a say—and I learned to live without him. Needless to say, that pain of losing my dad and the many questions I had, were pushed down for many years to come.

When my mom was forty years old she married Boone, who was thirty. She had five daughters and she was ten years older than him. Yup, my mom was a serious catch, and Boone turned out to be instrumental to me throughout my adolescence. He was also the reason I met many great people who would later land in my future.

When I was nine years old we moved, and I left a private school in Milwaukee that I felt extremely challenged in. When I tested in the Aspen schools I felt smart because I knew fractions in math, and Aspen school kids hadn't even started them in the fourth grade. They actually gave my mom a choice for me to go into fourth or fifth grade because it was 1979, let's remember. I chose fifth grade because the cute boy I knew was in that grade...seriously.

I wasn't an excellent student, but when I got to seventh grade I got the lead in the musical, *Cinderella*. I was thrilled and suddenly, just like that, I had found my thing! Growing up in Snowmass Village was magical. All of us who grew up in that valley still share stories and write about growing up in Aspen, well aware that we're a lucky bunch. I was hitchhiking around town, riding buses, selling newspapers, and making decent money as a thirteen-year-old. I had several jobs in the summers, consistently. I even started my own babysitting business at eleven years old with the help of my stepdad, Boone.

I graduated from Aspen High School in 1988. I was seventeen, and most of us couldn't wait to get the hell out of the small town we were in, which we referred to as the bubble. I left as fast as I could. I never looked back, although I consistently give the Aspen valley credit for my wonderful years and sacred memories of my childhood. When you're seventeen and feel like you've been cooped up, the grass is always greener on the other side.

I spent my first year of college at the University of Wisconsin-Milwaukee to be closer to my dad. I lived with him my first semester, in the dormitory the second semester, and then quickly exited after one year. I felt a strong pull to Los Angeles, where I moved in the summer of 1989. I first went to Long Beach and started school that year attempting to continue this acting and singing thing that I was addicted to. I turned nineteen in October of that year, and shortly after that I met Mike.

On the weekends I would drive an hour up to Beverly Hills to work for Neil Diamond and his family. I was helping out with their youngest child at the time while getting a taste of being a personal assistant. They were the best people to work for while I was also auditioning for commercials on the side and taking acting classes.

I was dating Mike at that time and he lived in North Hollywood while I was still in Long Beach. I saw him whenever I could on the weekends and eventually a lot more when I moved up to Burbank and started taking classes at UCLA. Working for the Diamonds turned into a full-time gig for me while I was a part-time student at UCLA. Mike and I were able to move into their guest house, and we got engaged in 1994 after five years of being together. It was great: two young people in love, able to save money and travel when my job needed us to. It was a young couple's dream, and the Diamonds were amazing to me.

In 1994 soon after Mike and I got engaged, I started a whole new career in the nightclub business working in the special events department. I also got a commercial agent, which allowed me to always be dabbling in commercial auditions and voice-over spots on the side. Mike and I got married in 1995, bought a house in 1996, and had our first child when Taylor came along in 2000 and then Emma in 2002. I stayed in that job for ten years while my kids were little, eventually running the special events department for two brothers and the three popular nightclubs they owned in Los Angeles. After working in that business for fourteen years, it was finally time for me to exit. I wanted to be a mom for a minute and revisit the acting/singing thing. I quickly fell back into working for Neil Diamond, and it was awesome. I was his personal assistant on the road when he was on tour. Obviously, that meant me traveling and leaving the girls with Mike, but Neil was supportive of me not being away from them longer than two weeks at a time. Either the girls would come to me, or I would fly home for two days, and then go back out on the road. We made it work.

My marriage had been gradually falling apart for years before that, so traveling was secretly a blessing for me. I know my absence was hard on the girls, but those years were the turning point for me. I knew I wasn't happy in my marriage, and being able to leave and explore the world for two to four weeks at a time was the dream. It was hard work, but most importantly I had a lot of time to get to know myself. Frankly, it's hard to admit that I missed the kids but not my husband. I knew it was happening. It was coming to an end, but it took me years to figure out how to actually end it.

I was fifteen years into a marriage, together twenty years with Mike. I had a great career, a beautiful home, and two beautiful, thriving daughters. However, I was going to sleep at night feeling completely alone. Mike and I had a really happy ten years together, and then things began to shift. Not in a good or bad way, but everything having to do with our relationship took a turn. I changed a lot over twenty years, and I personally discovered that we weren't all that great together. We didn't have much in common, and we did a lot of things on our own. When my mom and I were traveling with my kids more than Mike and I were, I knew there was no turning back. We were on and off in therapy for the entire twenty years together. I can't say we didn't *try* to fix it, because we did, but Mike and I separated in August of 2010.

Divorce. I will say that there is nothing easy, warm, or fuzzy about it. When two people who start out madly in love grow apart and have two children who want them together, divorce is sad and really difficult. It's worse than death in my opinion. My mom told me that—and she was spot on. Her saying that to me never resonated quite like it did until I was in the middle of one. If you're close to it or even entertaining the idea of divorce, just please try everything to make it work. In my opinion you'll be sorry if you don't, and I personally would do my best to talk you out of getting one. In all seriousness though, I believe there are a few reasons to get divorced. We had a big enough one to pull the trigger. I can tell you that it feels like a bullet in the heart to everyone involved.

With that said, four years later Taylor and Emma were adjusting well. I bought a new house in 2012 with my mom, who was my person. My house was a mile from our other one, and we were slowly adapting to the changes. I was working hard to stay afloat, support myself, pay my mortgage, and all the other things that come along with that. Mike and I shared custody of the girls and shared all their expenses as well. It felt like financial ruin for the first few years, but I had no regrets about leaving my marriage. I, of course, wish it could have worked out, but deep down I knew that wasn't going to happen. Bottom line is if you're not both willing to grow and do some work, then there's no saving it. There can't be one of you constantly waving a sign of trouble. The good news is Mike and I were amicable, and the girls were dealing well with two homes and the craziness of going back and forth. We were still being a family when we wanted to be and needed to be one. We were often spending holidays together, going to school functions, and Mike and I were co-parenting the best we could. Mike had a girlfriend and I had, well...I had my wonderful friends.

The night of Wednesday, June 4th was my first date in a long time that I was actually excited about: the date with Ryan (the one that never happened). I moved forward in life after 'that day' planning to be alone and convincing myself that I wouldn't be able to find any kind of meaningful relationship. I assumed no man could do it, and no man would want it. I forged ahead only fantasizing about having a true partner in life and in a marriage. I chose to live vicariously through the healthy relationships that I knew and was close to.

CHAPTER 6

Firstborn

On April 7th, 2000, the day Taylor was born, my life as I knew it changed forever. *Holy cow, I think this little human has it all figured out,* I thought to myself as I looked into that baby girl's eyes. She looked wise and relaxed, and we felt extremely comfortable with each other right away.

My pregnancy was easy, my delivery somewhat easy, and Taylor was an easy-going baby. She nursed well, slept well, and knew how to communicate with her dad and me. We knew the signals from day one, and because she was rarely fussy, we were able to roll with it.

Taylor didn't throw temper tantrums when she was a toddler, and she never once had to be removed from a public place for making a scene. She spoke early, memorized books at age two, and always loved an audience that would listen to her sing or read. She loved to perform. Thank goodness Emma came along two years later because she was willing to listen and be part of whatever Taylor had planned.

Taylor got one spanking from her dad when she was four years old. She started to go into the street to the neighbor's house without looking both ways. She only looked one way, and darted out. That never happened again.

Taylor was a joyful, cooperative, fun, and extremely loving child. When Taylor was four and Emma two, they were inseparable; and by the time Taylor was heading off to kindergarten, Emma would have done anything to join her. They constantly held hands, loved sharing bunk beds, wanted to dress alike, and could always be found building play set-ups in the living room. Always pretending. Having restaurants together and putting on concerts. It was constant entertainment for the adults.

What sticks out to me, is when Taylor was little, she would have crawled back into the womb if that choice had been offered to her. She and I were attached. Taylor preferred to be with certain people that she trusted, but especially didn't like to be away from me. When she started kindergarten it was an easy transition, partly because her dad taught PE at the school, but also because Taylor loved everything about it. She loved the teachers, loved to learn, and loved everything friendships had to offer. Taylor loved school *so* much that in first grade, she insisted on going to school even though she felt horrible and had a 104-degree temperature. Being that it was a rainy day, her dad and I pretended school was closed due to floods, which made her finally agree to stay home.

Taylor became a smart, driven, focused, and talented teenager. She loved her friends, and she loved anything to do with theater, music, and performing. Taylor had a lead in the sixth-grade play and sang a solo at sixth-grade graduation that was exquisite. She was coming into herself like no other teenager I knew. She had a memory that would often shock us, and she could memorize lines and lyrics in no time. She had a musical ear that the music teachers caught onto as well. She sang with a teacher and two high school seniors in a band for the first time when she was eight years old. Taylor was 'bitten by the bug,' as we say, and performed any chance she could get.

In eighth grade her class did a mock trial, and Taylor took it very seriously. She knocked it out of the park, and always found great joy in projects with her peers. That was the year

I saw her in what would be her last musical theater production. I was so proud of not only her natural talent but also her ability at such a young age to be such an empathetic and vulnerable actor. I'll never forget that last performance of hers and how I had no idea it would be her last. As a matter of fact, I thought exactly the opposite.

Taylor always wanted to be the best person she could be by helping others. It mattered to her if someone wasn't having a good day. Taylor was different in that way. Parents and teachers at school adored her because she would stop and say hello to them, learn their names, take time for them, and would genuinely enjoy doing it.

Taylor was always respectful of people and their feelings, especially her classmates. She said in the third grade, "I wish everyone could be friends with everyone. I just want everybody to get along."

Taylor respected friendships, and she hated any girl drama. She was consistently confident in who she was as a teenager, student, athlete, friend, mentor to younger children, and especially as an actress and a singer. Taylor had found her niche and gave it her all.

I know from a mom it might sound like I'm bragging about how wonderful she was. Trust me, she had her dark moments like any child or teenager, but there was something that made Taylor different. More importantly, I want you to know and understand what we lost in her.

CHAPTER 7

Our Premonition

I was feeding Taylor in my arms for what would be one of the last times when she was ten months old. It was a bonding fifteen minutes for us in the afternoon. Taylor and I didn't get these times often anymore because I was working full-time and trying to wean her completely from breast milk.

I was staring at her profile and thought, *Oh this sweet baby girl.* She often took my breath away. Her brown hair had grown out and she had sweet little curls that would lay on her face around her ocean-blue eyes. Her profile as I looked down at her was always so beautiful and perfect to me. I hoped that wouldn't change as she grew up. It was a quiet afternoon, no one else was home, and as I watched her, I took every inch of her in. How she smelled, what she felt like, how big she was getting right before my eyes, and how much I completely loved her.

I had wanted children for as long as I could remember. When I was seven years old, I had eighteen imaginary children that would come alive to me when I was alone. I didn't realize then that having these eighteen imaginary kids meant that I was really craving to be a mother. I certainly realize it now. Deep down I knew I was here to be a mom, and there I was looking down at my beautiful girl.

As I held Taylor in my arms in our living room, I had many different feelings running through me. By being born, Taylor had fulfilled one of my childhood wishes of being a mom. I marveled at her sweetness and at the incredible human that she was becoming right in front of my eyes. The one constant between the two of us was our outgoing personalities. Taylor was always greeting people even as a toddler. I couldn't take her anywhere without her constantly saying "hiiiiiiiiii" to complete strangers once they locked eyes with her. Errands were always delayed because of people stopping to interact, say hello to her, or comment on her poise and manners at such a young age.

At a year old, Taylor was talking. At fourteen months she knew the names of all her Velcro plastic vegetables, her ABCs, numbers, and a lot of kitchen items. She always listened intently and loved to be a parrot and repeat absolutely everything (including "goddamnit"). Since she was my first child, I had accepted her verbal ability as normal. I only realized it was unusual when other parents would get upset because their child was still saying "nana" and Taylor would correct them and say, "No no no, that's a BAnana." We never got called again for playdates with those kids.

As I held her in my arms that warm afternoon I made gentle circles on her head. Thinking about her sponge-like brain that was constantly making connections with the world around her and soaking it all in. Out of nowhere I suddenly felt this great need to protect her brain. I had always been flooded with love as I held her in these moments, but this time was different. This time the primary emotion was responsibility. I started feeling desperate as I started praying to God, the universe, and all the higher powers to look after this baby girl of mine. Specifically her precious brain as I stroked her head. It is everything in the growth of a child, and I was fascinated by it.

I was gazing at her profile deep in thought when Taylor abruptly pulled away from me. Her blue eyes were terrified and soft whimpering was coming out of her mouth. She immediately started crying. It was different from how she usually cried. I looked behind me because it was as if she had seen something that frightened her. As I remember it, her cry began as a bewildered whimpering, it grew progressively stronger, and the only way I can explain it is that it turned into a screaming *I'm really frightened* kind of cry. I grabbed her body quickly to calm her. I wanted her to stop crying, and how I wished she could talk to me. Instead, Taylor grabbed my shirt and hurled herself into my chest.

"What is it, baby?" I asked her. Now I was frightened as well and started to tear up. I didn't understand what was happening. Why was she so scared? And why did I suddenly feel fear? I also started to cry but quickly wiped my tears so it wouldn't scare her more. I held her as tightly as she did me, and I rocked back and forth to calm both of us. After a few minutes of soothing her, I assured her she was okay and said over and over in her ear, "It's okay, baby, it's gonna be okay. Mama's here, I'm here. Mama's gotcha."

I can't tell you how many times I have gone back to this scene. My feeling of helplessness coupled with responsibility. Did Taylor have a vision of some kind? Did she get a glance at what was going to happen to her? I'll never really know.

All I can tell you is that one sunny afternoon on another day, in another part of the city, my daughter's brain was injured. Like I had promised her when she was a baby, in the hospital 'that day' I whispered in her ear again, "It's okay baby, it's gonna be okay. Mama's gotcha."

I had hoped I would never have to make good on that promise in this way. But I've often thought that perhaps the connections forged all those years ago between Taylor and me, is what helped us 'that day' in the emergency room. Maybe it helped me see what she would need. It's certainly what got me through the next sixty-six days of Taylor being in the hospital.

CHAPTER 8

The Dream

On March 4th, 2014, exactly three months before Taylor was hit by the car, she came to breakfast that morning begging me to write her a note for school so she would be able to skip her PE classes for the rest of the year. As Taylor ate her toast and fruit she explained how she didn't like PE class. She told me she despised it and didn't want to do it anymore. She continued to share that she hadn't slept that well because of a bad dream, but she couldn't remember the dream or any details about it. She was only adamant that she didn't want to do PE class anymore.

Taylor seemed desperate to have a note to excuse her from that class, but I brushed it off as her being a lazy teen. Both girls knew the morning routine, and with her carpool coming to pick her up in thirty minutes, Taylor knew better than to be stalling. After listening to her argument, I was able to distract her and then wrote her this note:

> Dear PE class,
> Taylor needs to skip PE today.
> Oh and every day for the rest of the school year.
> Just because. Thanks so much. ☺
> Laurel

When Taylor read the note she was thrilled and relieved. "Mom, really?...Is this for real?" she asked.

"Well, if you give it to your teacher, what do you think he'll say?" I asked her.

She smiled. "He'll probably laugh."

"He sure will, but you can give it to him," I told her.

Now anyone who knows me well, knows that the note was a joke, and I wouldn't let either one of my girls get out of something because they didn't feel like doing it. However, the note served as a nice distraction because Taylor went off to school and PE that morning without mentioning it again. Because the whole thing was hilarious to me, I posted a picture of the note on Facebook at 8:32 am with this caption:

> If I let her do it,
> she said I'll be the BEST MOM EVER.
> Dear PE class,
> Please be sure to kick her ass.

That was my post. Yup, I said it, and boy it *sure* did.

Since Taylor was crossing the street on June 4th with her PE class, don't think I haven't thought back to that note I wrote, because I have. I've thought long and hard about it. I think it strange that Taylor had a restless night and couldn't fully explain her dream to me, but I also feel horrible inside for telling PE to do that to her. In more ways than one, I regret it. To rewind, oh wait...that's not a thing.

Thinking about that morning scenario later that afternoon, I couldn't understand why Taylor was reacting like that to volleyball. She was really good at it, she loved playing, and the whole family went to her games to cheer her on. They were also a winning team, so who wouldn't love being a part of that? Taylor knew volleyball and had been playing it since sixth grade with her classmates. It was definitely unusual behavior to me. I mean, it wasn't track and field where the kids had to run miles and miles.

Taylor was always eager to go to school and play sports and now this. There was reluctance to go to school that particular day, and it was certainly out of the ordinary. She was anxious and acting out by fighting with her sister, defying me a little more often, and behaving differently. Taylor had recently started changing the way she was eating. She was making much healthier choices in her school lunch: no junk food, not eating as much sugar, drinking a lot of water, and cutting out soda completely. She made it clear to me that she was working hard to be strong for volleyball. I had also noticed a pretty serious crush on a boy in her grade for the first time. They were having phone conversations and planning to do things together. When she started changing the way she was eating and becoming a little teenagery, I started to wonder if this was what everyone was talking about with teenage girls. They get chips on their shoulders, are surly, easily agitated with you, and flat-out bitchy. I attributed Taylor's attitude change to the stress of ending eighth grade. After all, in June she would no longer be in middle school, and come September, there would be a lot more pressure academically in high school. It all mattered in high school. Or at least that's what you think when you're fourteen.

In the afternoon on Sunday, June 1st, 2014, three days before that fateful day, Taylor and Emma had gotten into the biggest fight of their lives. I was in the kitchen doing dishes when I heard shouting from the girls' bathroom. I gave it a moment because they would usually resolve it. I heard it escalate to another level quickly. I went in and heard Taylor screaming at Emma about being on her side of the counter, and Emma was cowering over the bathtub as Taylor was taking a swing at her. Emma looked completely freaked out and ducked under me to escape Taylor and run into her room. The two of them had had little bickers before this, but this argument was mean and nasty. Taylor said some things to

Emma that I knew she would regret later. Taylor was completely out of line and extremely mean, and hours later I was still being the peacekeeper. After awhile, I could still hear Taylor badgering Emma about what happened earlier in the bathroom. We were all getting ready to go somewhere, and I told Taylor to take some time in her room by herself until we were ready to get in the car. I'm quite sure it had been ten years since the last time I had to put her in a time-out.

They ignored each other during and after our outing. I knew this was not going to blow over quickly, and I wasn't going to let that argument shape our next five days together. Emma came to me later that evening still feeling hurt and confused about not only Taylor's reaction but her sheer anger. I sensed Emma was a little scared of Taylor, which prompted the little pow-wow that came next.

The past month, I had sensed a sudden change in Taylor and noticed she was stressed. She was a good student and was suddenly anxious about her grades and her exams coming up. She had also been spending more time in her room by herself. Now this fight with her sister that even Emma couldn't understand? I sat down on Taylor's bed, uninvited of course, and asked if there was anything I could do to help her. We've always had a close relationship, but it was feeling strained. I wanted to give her the chance to share her feelings with me and let me in, but she quickly told me to leave her room. I stayed without exiting because you're not allowed to excuse me from your room when I'm your mom. I proceeded to remind Taylor that she only had one sister. One sister who will be there for her when her dad and I are gone someday. One sister to rely on. I started to cry because I desperately needed to communicate this to her. Through my tears, I explained to Taylor that we are her family and she is not allowed to treat Emma so miserably. I told her she needed to change her attitude toward me especially, and could not continue this behavior toward us. I explained that we are the people who love her the most, and we are here to support her, not be her enemies. Taylor didn't stop me. I kept spewing and found myself telling her that I was not always going to be here on this planet—to talk, to listen, and to help her—because one day (hopefully before her) I will die.

And if she continues like this, her sister will be living her own life someday, not speaking to her. I told Taylor that I wanted her to be close to me and Emma. Remember the three Musketeers that we are? Taylor started to cry and apologized as she sobbed. I will never forget her saying not only how sorry she was, but that she didn't understand why she was behaving this way. Taylor confessed that she wasn't feeling like herself, and at the end of that conversation, the two of us thought her changes were due to end-of-year stress. We created some ideas on how to approach that for the next week and through her upcoming finals. I certainly didn't expect the strategies we discussed then, would turn into helping her fight for her life.

Journal Entry Day 14
June 17th, 2014

I think today I miss Taylor's smile the most. She had a couple wakeful moments with a look on her face that was between disgust and confusion. Kinda funny, but it didn't suit her really, so hopefully she'll be smiling again soon.

Taylor gets her surgery tomorrow around 5 pm for her mickey button feeding tube, which means no more tubes through her nose. Her pelvic fracture is healing slowly but well, and all the other little things like bruises and scrapes are slowly starting to fade away. Just in time for Taylor to slowly start coming back.

Still not much movement on her right side, and we know

it's going to be awhile. We're now looking at what the next three to six months look like for us: where we'll go next, the care she needs, and her rehabilitation. I will send updates, because after dissecting it, I know that's where we'll need you all the most.

My mom is here from Colorado right now to be with me, and she's a blessing.

Journal Entry Day 15
June 18th, 2014

Once again I am comforted and moved by your compassion and love for Taylor. Your thoughts, prayers, and positive energy are seeping through your words, and I hang onto each and every one tightly.

Taylor went in for surgery at 5:45 this evening and all went well. She is still feeling a little groggy from it, but for the most part it was a breeze. She is in good hands here, and what I'm realizing is every single staff member in the Kaiser LA Hospital that we've encountered knows Taylor's story by now. The compassion they all show has floored me. Especially today. Each and every volunteer, nurse, doctor, resident, anesthesiologist, and surgeon is doing everything they can to accommodate her. It's amazing and powerful stuff. I bow to them and thank them a million times over.

Taylor's still sleeping a lot and in wakeful moments was more agitated today. Her eyes are opening wider each day, and these are great baby steps. I'm pretty sure today when I was putting chapstick on her lips after her bath I got a little smirk out of her. It made me smile.

My mom is still here and I am grateful for each day she can be here with me. Today is also Emma's twelfth birthday, which also makes me smile. Happy Birthday to my sweet Emma.

Journal Entry Day 16
June 19th, 2014

Before I write in this journal, I make sure to catch up on your notes. I'm grateful to all of you. For the boys in Taylor's class who are trekking for Taylor in the mountains. For all of you who have taken this on with us.

Today was exhausting for Mike and me on so many levels because it was a big day. We will be moving to a different hospital soon in order to get Taylor the care she needs before she's ready for any kind of rehab process. That move might be as soon as Saturday, and like our first move, it will be hard to leave this place. We will go to a children's hospital that specializes in this kind of injury, and you know as well as I do she'll win all their hearts. We will keep you all posted on the move and let you know when visitors and her friends are welcome. We'll be there awhile, but this next move will be a big step in Taylor's recovery.

They started her feeds today through her mic-key button, and all is going well. I know for a fact she's happy to have that tube out of her nose. She was awake with eyes open today for a total of one hour. It's a longer stretch of time than other days, which is a good sign, and she's beginning to swallow which is really important progress. It's a really big (baby) step, as crazy as that sounds.

Please keep sending love, and I'll keep visualizing Taylor's brain cables and nerves reconnecting and firing. In case you didn't hear, blue is now called Taylor Blue 'round here. It started with kids at their school all wearing blue one day in support of all three girls hit by the car. So paint those nails and rock that color in any way you can!

part
three

CHAPTER 9

The Bridge

Taylor's dad and I were speaking with hospital social workers regarding where Taylor would go next. This was day sixteen, and she was in the pediatric wing at the Kaiser hospital. Taylor was slowly becoming alert in the sense that her eyes could be open for a total of forty-five minutes a day, and in a fleeting moment, she might make eye contact with you. Taylor needed to start getting therapies regularly. Speech therapy, occupational therapy, and physical therapy. I was told to move her limbs as much as I could when I was with her, and we all pitched in to do that.

When therapists tried to sit Taylor up for the first time in her bed, it all became very real to me. It took two therapists, all of us slowly talking her through it, and thirty-two minutes to physically get her body into a seated position. She was excruciatingly uncomfortable, and because she wasn't even swallowing correctly, gravity became an interesting factor in the process as well. I stood back at one point to get a look at her, and even with the therapists holding her up, she looked like a marionette with no one holding her strings. She had no strength, no muscle control at all, and it was like sitting up was completely foreign to her. She was slumped over, drooling, and shaking while her body was fighting being vertical in every way. Taylor's face looked scared and extremely unsure of what was going on. That moment was when I understood the amount of help Taylor was going to need. I started to get emotional watching a strong man and woman struggle with her the way they had.

It was like watching a baby in an uncooperative fourteen-year-old body who had to learn everything over again. Even though her body wasn't ready to sit up, we had to do it every day in therapy from now on. Taylor was exhausted after the last forty-five minutes, and slept the rest of the day.

I felt deeply disturbed by all of it and had to let everything that I just witnessed process inside me. It was hard, really hard to watch my once athletic, active, strong child struggle that much to simply sit up. It was from that moment forward I knew none of this was going to be easy. I also knew that physically (for me) it was going to be a challenge, and we needed to find the best transition hospital to help all of us get through this next stage.

HealthBridge Children's Hospital became my number-one pick for where we would go next. If there was a bed open, our insurance was willing to give us one hundred days in that facility. A win! After speaking to the director of the hospital and going down to Orange County to look at it, I knew it was the place for Taylor. It was perfect. A bed was going to open up for Taylor within three days' time (another win)! Finally...

· · ·

Then a slight bump in the road. Mike and I were meeting with doctors and social workers to discuss what Taylor's transfer would look like, when exactly it would happen, and what might get accomplished in those one hundred days at HealthBridge Children's Hospital. We also discussed what might happen *after* one hundred days and what bringing Taylor home might look like.

Most everyone had cleared the room when Mike pulled me aside and told me that he wanted to consider taking

Taylor home. I wasn't sure where this was coming from, but I did think he was reaching for anything that might make this easier, more comfortable, or make it go faster. I wasn't really sure. What I *did* know was that I couldn't possibly take care of Taylor at home. In all honesty, I knew that I would have to be her main caretaker and not her dad. I couldn't possibly do that by myself, and a nurse, twenty-four hours a day to help me was certainly not in the budget. Frustrated, I reminded Mike that Taylor couldn't sit up, roll over, speak, eat, or even move at this point. She was completely incontinent (in diapers) and needed constant care. As I was saying these things to him, I thought it would surely click and he would respond by saying, "Never mind Laurel, you're right. Going home is not a possibility yet." But he didn't say that, and was adamant about wanting her to come home.

I left the room to pace the hallway for a few minutes to think on this insane idea of his. I certainly wasn't ready to take care of Taylor at home, and I was annoyed he would even think it could be possible at this point. Especially because I knew I would be the main caretaker. I was so angry. I also suddenly felt challenged on what we had been discussing with her team all along.

I immediately went right down to the office of the social worker who had been in that meeting and told her what Mike was thinking. She, of course, was shocked and gave me some advice. If he was truly wanting to do this, I would have to get support from doctors and professionals and basically tell her father what was going to happen. If he didn't agree, then it was suggested to me that I get an attorney, and fight him on it. The social worker also informed me that once we discharge her from the hospital (as parents of a minor), our health insurance would not support her if we had to bring her back.

With that information, and me seething inside, I let the

day and afternoon go by. Without calling an attorney, I told Mike the following morning what I had learned. "It's not the ideal option," I told him and then said, "I will be arranging our move down to HealthBridge Hospital with Taylor. You can come or not. It's your choice."

Mike listened, looked down, shook his head yes and said, "Okay."

Bump in the road: dealt with.

* * *

I understand now where Mike was coming from. Some men want to fix things, and they'll do whatever it takes to make it look or feel fixed. Women can sometimes be more patient and understand the process of things more deeply. That little glitch for Mike and me made me realize that I had to really be on point with the medical facts of the situation, the health insurance policies, and the system as a whole. I had to understand the details, and I had to get other opinions and options for almost everything that was going to happen from now on. That meant most of the work was mine, and I knew it after this incident had happened. I was going to be her main advocate, and there was little room for mistakes.

* * *

When we got to HealthBridge I took a giant deep breath. The nurses were so helpful and everyone was kind and compassionate, especially with Taylor. I knew this was a special place we had entered into, and I also had an overwhelming, beautiful feeling that this might be our last stop. A long one, but our last. Our bridge to home, hopefully.

Journal Entry Day 18
June 21st, 2014

We made it! Mike and I moved Taylor to the new hospital early this morning. We spent the whole day here together getting our tour and meeting the main doctors and nursing staff. We were learning the ropes and rules, which I'm convinced Taylor will surely break at some point.

Once again, getting out of the ambulance she absolutely loved being outside. We hope to do that a lot in her new place of healing. HealthBridge is a one-story hospital that is more like a ranch-style home. They have a front porch, a backyard, and sidewalks all around for wheelchair rides. She'll be happy here. Today, we begin the next part of her journey, today being the beginning of the summer solstice. Here's to beautiful and powerful new beginnings.

Taylor has been exhausted these last couple of days, but we're letting her rest because Monday brings on a lot of work for her. Meeting a lot of new people, and hopefully beginning some therapy sessions in between her fatigue. This place is wonderful, and she will thrive here. It also helps that there is a Target store close by.

We consider ourselves fortunate to have gotten her into this hospital, and as hard as some moments may be, behind us and ahead of us, this move brings us that much closer to getting her home.

Journal Entry Day 19
June 22nd, 2014

Yesterday was a big day for us. Mike and I will be alternating every forty-eight hours living at HealthBridge with Taylor in her room. I think it will be hard every time one of us has to leave; however, it allows us to really focus on our job when we're here.

Last night and today, Taylor and I spent a lot of time settling in, and preparing for what's ahead. We're talking to her a lot about what is happening in her brief wakeful moments. I'm hoping she's processing it little by little. I'm mindful about staying positive and constantly reassuring her that all will be well. I know she's confused at times, and I can't imagine what that feels like for her. Having no words at all.

She hooks her left arm around me now, and I keep telling her how much we all love her. I am certain that the most important thing (besides being here) is that Mike and I are with her every step of the way.

Taylor doesn't have an IV or anything else sticking in her now. Only her mic-key button which everything is administered through. We're thrilled about that, and eating through her mouth will hopefully come at some point. She will be evaluated tomorrow, and therapy sessions will be starting soon. I love this little hospital and its mission statement:

> To provide the highest quality of care
> to medically fragile children
> and their families in a homelike environment
> while facilitating a judicious transition home.

What a beautiful place, and how lucky we are that Taylor is here.

Mike's Journal Entry Day 20
June 23rd, 2014

Eric Clapton once said, "Lately, I've been running on faith." And I know exactly what those words mean now. Thank you to all of you who continue to follow Taylor through this journey; your love and support are a constant source of strength right now. Taylor continues to amaze me with her strength and courage. It was so heartwarming to see Taylor and Laurel cuddling in bed today: poor thing was sooooo confused, but comforted in the loving arms of her mother. I cried all the way home, alternating between hope and fear, listening to the words in that song. Until tomorrow.

Journal Entry Day 21
June 24th, 2014

I was speaking to the director of the hospital today and she wanted me to tell her about Taylor. She asked me what Taylor is like, what kind of person she is, what she loves, hobbies or activities, and some of her favorite things. After summing up Taylor to her, I tried to describe Taylor's essence and her genuine, beautiful spirit. It wasn't easy to get the words out—but as a mother, if someone asks you to do that, sort of 'in remembrance' it certainly makes you pause. I am grateful for who she is and I'd give anything to have her back someday. I know she has more to show this world regarding who she is, so we'll wait.

Taylor had her first therapy session today. Speech therapy for her to start learning how her mouth works again. They took my advice from yesterday and tried chocolate pudding instead of applesauce (which she's hated her whole life), and it worked! Chocolate pudding it is. More tomorrow.

Emma and I are sleeping a lot while enjoying the pleasures of home.

Journal Entry Day 22
June 25th, 2014

Three weeks since 'that day:' the day that will forever be life-changing to all of us.

Taylor's strength has improved immensely in the last couple of weeks, because I remember (too vividly) watching two strong nurses attempt to sit her up. Things have changed since then. Taylor can sit up, move around, kick, and punch with her left arm. She can also tell you what she wants with her body, which most of the time is, *get me out of this bed, this room, and this place right this instant,* without her actually being able to say the words. When these 'brain storms' hit her, she immediately connects with that fight or flight mode (that all of our brains know), and she wants out. When her brain makes a connection now there is an instantly fired reaction, and it isn't always the correct one. 'Brain storms' are rough, and we have no idea what those look like inside her mind. Taylor makes it clear to us (every day) that she wants out of this place.

Mike and I will be working extra hard now.

We have to believe that if Taylor keeps on showing the strength and healing that she has in this last week that she is going to make quite a comeback at some point. She is determined and gets frustrated at times, but I see a fight in her eyes, a fire. I'm hoping that we, as her team, can stay focused, hopeful, positive, strong, and courageous as the hardest part of this journey begins.

Today this journey became all too real for me. I was remembering that three short weeks ago our morning started out as a normal school day. Now our lives are—well—different let's say. Taylor will be my job, and I am determined to help her. I don't know what that looks like, but I will do whatever it takes to get the job done. As we settle into our new routine, and I meet Taylor's therapists, I know we're all going to dig in and give it our best. GO, Taylor, GO (is my new motto).

Journal Entry Day 26
June 29th, 2014

I wasn't going to write a post today, and then I thought it was important. Mike and I are thrilled when something new happens every day as Taylor's brain pieces back together.

However, today was a sad day for Emma. She had a fun morning with friends and then came home to reality. The reality that this horrific thing has happened to her sister, to Taylor, and to us. She misses her sister and feels bad that Taylor has to be where she is. Emma is confused about this journey we're on, as a lot of us are, and she is also scared to see Taylor. I'm happy that Emma's talking, opening up, and crying and feeling it, but it still makes a mother's heart ache in double time. And that ache is sometimes hard to soothe.

Emma is only twelve, and this is big stuff to wrap your head around. That goes for all of our precious children involved.

On a lighter note, Emma also mentioned moving to Colorado to live in a treehouse (which doesn't sound all that crazy to me).

I know that we all miss Taylor, and I know a lot of this is hard to explain. Please hold my Emma close to your hearts and send her good thoughts. She needs you.

Journal Entry Day 30
July 3rd, 2014

First thing this morning, I told Emma about Taylor climbing out of her bed yesterday and crawling to the door to escape out of her room. Taylor was quickly busted by her dad and a nurse, but Emma's comment was, "Wow! That's awesome!"

At the doctors, meeting on Tuesday, I was told it will start to get very interesting. I'm pretty sure the escape episode is what they meant by that. They also assured me that what she will do is nothing they haven't seen before. (But I'm quite sure Taylor will do something they haven't seen before.) All kidding aside, Taylor's spirit is strong and we all know it. I feel it when I'm with her, hovering over us. We know she's working hard putting everything back together in her brain. When she has moments of connection it's hard to know what she's thinking, with no voice to express herself. I know it must be terrifying for her because I see it in her eyes. I hope she'll be able to tell us something soon.

Journal Entry Day 31
July 4th, 2014

Exactly one month since 'that day' and how appropriate for it to be the day we celebrate our independence and freedom. Today as I watched Taylor struggle with the fact that she's not quite ready to be independent again, I saw her want it more than anything. It's a difficult struggle for her, and I can see it in her eyes. After getting very upset and crying at one point, she did over seventy sit-ups thinking she was getting out of bed. Super determined, then confused, and more than frustrated when I was there to stop her. After trying to knock two nurses down with her left-leg sidekick while trying to escape over her bed rails, Taylor's room now looks like a CrossFit training center with mats everywhere. Safety first, and workout clothes are now my uniform.

Christine is Taylor's speech therapist who is eight months pregnant, and during their session today I had to hold up a mat to protect her from Taylor's swings. Taylor was exhausted afterward but wound up giving Christine a nice wave goodbye.

Claire, my yoga guru, texted me earlier today and said, "Celebrating Taylor today and her re-finding her inner dependence."

Beautiful words. I will continue to celebrate Taylor in working hard to find herself again. What I have learned is that this all takes determination. In order to make it back to independence it takes want, it takes courage, and it takes hunger. Those who have those things are the ones that make it back. I'm quite sure Taylor is one of them.

Happy Independence Day to all of you. Here's to the red, white, and Taylor BLUE. I'm gonna go rest on a gym mat now.

CHAPTER 10

Moving Forward

I was feeling exhausted by hospital day five, but especially by hospital day THIRTY-five. Days with Taylor at HealthBridge were becoming not only draining, but they were also lonely and isolating. She still wasn't speaking, and communicating with her was getting more and more difficult. One of the most challenging things was changing her diaper. Sometimes it would take three of us (six hands) to finish the task.

Most days I couldn't wait for therapy sessions, meal times, or even a visit from someone. Walking down the hall to the communal kitchen to get a cup of coffee was sometimes the highlight of an hour or two, and I was really lucky if I got to eat a decent meal. Taylor wasn't resting as much as she used to, and when she was awake it was getting harder and harder to keep her busy and entertained. She couldn't walk, and she still had no words and was not able to properly communicate with us. She was often frustrated, and outbursts of aggression were happening several times a day.

I was able to use Taylor's bathroom in her room at night to take a shower after I had her tucked into bed. I would literally tuck her sheets and blanket tightly around her like a straight jacket. Too many times before I did this, she would look asleep and then suddenly sit up to try and get out of bed. If you were with her, no matter what time of day, you had to always be watching. Her newest thing was this: she would sit up in bed, reach out to you for a hug, and then use your body for momentum to get over the bed rail. My back hurt, my legs ached, and I was exhausted. It was much like having a crawling, curious toddler again. Except she was a strong gigantic one.

It had been a long day and an unusually difficult night getting Taylor settled. She had kicked me in the thigh really hard that morning, and I noticed a huge bruise starting to form. I was sore all over my body, and couldn't wait to get in the shower. Whenever you used her bathroom though, no matter what business you were taking care of, you had to leave the bathroom door open wide enough to still be able to see her. Always fun when nurses (male and female) would drop in at any moment. You learn early on in this environment that it's best to put your inhibitions aside and try to roll with it. Two days prior at the doctors' meeting, I had asked if we could be alone with Taylor after 9 pm in order to get a full night's sleep. Nurses were coming in every four hours to check on her, and it wasn't necessary at that point. The noise from the double doors was the most disruptive when they closed, and my sleep was like bags of gold at that point. I assured them I was able to handle her, and if necessary I would push the red-call-button for their help if needed. My little bed that folded into a chair during the day was wedged right up next to hers so she could never get past me. They agreed, and for the past two nights we had gotten privacy, quiet, and two solid nights of sleep.

When Taylor was finally settled in bed, I got in the shower and stood under the warm water for quite a while. I put shampoo in my hair and was of course watching Taylor with one eye open. You always had to be ready to abort your mission and possibly go after her. As I was staring at her through the cracked door I started to cry. I felt the weight of the day and everything on me. I desperately wanted her to talk to me, I wanted and needed this to get easier. As I fell to the shower floor, I wasn't sure I could do this anymore. I needed to take her home and get the hell out of here. I wanted my Taylor back, and I needed something to help me get through this.

I was pleading, crying, gasping for air, and having a breakdown—and yes, that's exactly what was happening to me. I felt it deep down in my chest. Even though I was attempting to cry quietly, it wasn't working. I sat on the floor of the shower and let it out. I was scared. I was mad, and I needed something to finally give. It had been so many days of doing the same thing, and I desperately wanted to go home. All I kept thinking was, *I need some kind of sign or something that I can hold on to because I'm starting to lose my grip.* Something had to change or I wasn't sure I'd be able to hang in there. The more I thought of Taylor and what she used to be like, the harder I would sob. I didn't recognize my own daughter, I didn't recognize myself, I missed my life, and I didn't want to spend one more day in that hospital playing Groundhog Day.

"I hate this," I sobbed, "Please, I need something to help me!" I asked out loud. I wasn't sure who I was talking to, but I put it out there and then slowly started to piece myself back together. I went to bed next to Taylor feeling sad and lonely for the first time since we had been there. I didn't like that, and I knew in the morning I had to start with calling some friends. I slept really well that night, and I'm quite sure Taylor did too.

Journal Entry Day 36
July 9th, 2014

Today was an excellent day! Today I am on my knees in gratitude.

This morning it began with nods from Taylor on her own; and then with some help, she found her voice and connected it with words! Christine, her pregnant speech therapist, helped Taylor find her "yes" and her "no" words today. She then went on to ask Taylor a series of yes or no questions. Taylor knows she's not a man, and she knows she doesn't have three eyes, and she also knows she doesn't live in Wisconsin—but California got a "YES!"

Then, with some humming and coaxing came "Maaaaaa-oooom" and then, "Hiiiiii, mooom," and then slowly, "I love you, Mommy," as she reached out to hug me.

I fell to my knees at the side of her bed shedding the happiest tears of my entire life. Neither Christine nor I were expecting that to happen, and we were both thrilled. Then Taylor said, "Hello, my name is Taylor." (Feeling the need to introduce herself nineteen times after that.) She also identified a few things with words: hairbrush, hairspray, and EOS lip balm! Yes, that is what she said.

Taylor laid down looking exhausted after that particular fifteen minutes, and I looked at her and asked, "How are you?"

She closed her eyes, opened them up after a nice long pause, and then in true Taylor fashion said, "Good, how are you?"

I told her through happy tears, "I am so good Taylor. And I'm thrilled you decided to talk to us today."

We called her dad on the phone and I put Taylor on speaker phone so he could hear her say "I love you." Mike was over the moon.

To top it off, later in the day Taylor stood up (mostly having to use her left leg), but she was standing on her own two feet for the first time. Her physical therapist, Jenn, talked her through it with much encouragement, and Taylor was proud. She leaned against Jenn for a full minute of standing while they looked each other in the eye, spoke some words I couldn't hear, and shared some giggles. They have sealed their bond.

My heart is filled as I continue to be hopeful, grateful, and mindful as all of this slowly unfolds before us. I will continue to pray for patience, understanding, and strength. I will continue to lean on all of you for support and courage. Thank you. Each of you. Today was an excellent day. An excellent day indeed.

I definitely got my *something to help me* on that incredible day.

Journal Entry Day 39
July 12th, 2014

I had hoped for the gift of guidance coming my way last night, and now I know why.

It was a day of mixed emotions. Once Taylor was fully awake this morning I heard the first "Hello, my name is Elder Price..." come out of her. I wanted to laugh, but couldn't because she looked like a deer-in-headlights. I told Mike, since he had seen this happen, that I thought she was remembering the day of the accident. I was told she was singing as they were walking back to school on June 4th. *The Book of Mormon* is one of her favorite Broadway musicals. Taylor kept saying this all day, and her occupational therapist agreed she had that deer-in-headlights look when she would repeat it over and over almost frantically. Taylor's sound has a similar tone to a deaf person who can speak, so we're working on that and also getting her hearing checked.

For those of you who don't know, Taylor loves her Broadway show tunes and has been especially intrigued with *The*

Book of Mormon lately. Her repeating that one line from the show continued all day: even during speech therapy as she practiced what day it is, the month, and counting how old she is. The line would always be peppered in, and we tried to ignore her repeating it.

Taylor doesn't really rest during the day much anymore, so you have to constantly be pulling something out of your bag of tricks. She did a lot of exercises with Mom today on the floor. She's on her phone a lot now too, so I'm sorry to those of you who received texts that looked a little something like this today "#$%#(%?!@%." She means well.

I did offer to type for her, and at one point she wanted me to text someone, "What happened?" She got demanding and started repeating to me, "What happened, what happened, what happened?" (Again, frantic.)

Today, Taylor reminds me a lot of Dory (from *Finding Nemo*) with her short-term memory being so horrible, and she's also a lot like Raymond from the movie *Rain Man*. Two common characters to resemble when your brain is sorting through all of this. Dory forgets a lot, and Rain Man needs to be routine and repetitive. Her brain is re-firing, re-wiring, re-organizing, and most importantly, attempting to remember everything she used to know. I suspect Dory and Rain Man will be here for a while.

Taylor's neck and back have been bothering her, and she's able to voice it now, which is helpful. I was massaging her neck as she was sitting up before dinnertime and Taylor looked straight ahead and said very matter-of-factly, "Hello my name is Elder Price, and I was in the park!"

I looked at her and told her she was right. I have never mentioned that detail of 'that day' to her, so I knew what was happening. I softly began telling her some details of what happened. I then explained where we are now, how long it's been, and why we're here. She shook her head yes, and laid her head on my shoulder. She stayed there a while as I held her. No words needed. We stayed quiet as I thought she was possibly piecing it all together.

Dory will most likely need that information again and again, but it's slowly coming together. Makes it extra tricky for me and I'm extra tired, but I'm going to see this process through. The wonderful thing is that Taylor's alive. She's doing everything she can to understand it all quickly: where June went, what the heck happened, where we are and why. She's doing it with frustration, concern, pain, agitation, sadness, and smiles. She will figure this out eventually.

Journal Entry Day 43
July 16th, 2014

Taylor has changed a lot in the past forty-eight hours. She woke up this morning, saw me, and said, "Good morning."

Her inflection is not quite back yet, but there is no doubt that her loving kindness is. She thanked her nurse, Amy, for her shot in the stomach this morning.

Amy knows and adores her, and while laughing, replied, "You're welcome Taylor. I'm pretty sure I have never gotten a thank you for that before."

What's happening now is this: just as the doctor said, the long-term filing cabinets in her brain are all intact. We know this because she knows some Spanish and details about her childhood. Things that have been in there long-term. Moving forward with Taylor or any brain-injured person, helping them open the drawers of those file cabinets is imperative. Then she'll need to sort through all the information on her own time. Her brain has to somehow connect all of it back together. Being able to help them open the filing drawers in order to have the information is key. Then sorting through all of it will most likely be difficult, tiring, and frustrating. I know it is for Taylor. Her agitation is beginning to subside a bit, as we all encourage her to take her time. She is busy opening the drawers and sorting. It's like you can see it happening in her eyes. I can imagine the unorganized information being overwhelming right now.

We're really working on Taylor starting to move her right side. Her right hand is frustrating to her during therapy, but we're always encouraging her to find it, use it, and love it. We tempted her today by practicing a small volleyball serve on her knees with a beach ball. Taylor used to play a lot of volleyball, and I could see in her eyes that she really wanted to hit it.

Dory and Rain Man come and go a lot, and they are frequently here at the same time together. Taylor insisted on wearing surgical gloves all morning. I kind of like it when they both come to visit, because it's my comedy relief.

Taylor also asked Amy, "Amy, please go talk to someone you work with to find my release date, and then bring it to me, okay?"

Yup. Amy, you heard the boss; that's what she wants. Thanks so much, Amy, and thank goodness Amy and I can both laugh hysterically in private.

And now for the best part of our day. We were watching a *Glee* episode on DVD, and I was sitting right next to her on her bed. Taylor grabbed my arm at one point, and I looked up at her. She went into full performance mode, and for a moment I couldn't believe my eyes. She was mouthing the words to me with theatrical emotion in her eyes and face. Only her sound was missing, but I was watching her perform. I quickly joined her and we lip-synced the chorus to each other using plastic spoons as microphones. "I'll Stand By You" by The Pretenders. A great song.

Taylor didn't miss a single word, a single beat, or a riff! That was a tough song for me to get through, but I knew I had to stay in it with her. You see, Taylor's not liking the sound of her own singing voice these days. She stayed mute and mouthed the words because her voice in general sounds different, especially her singing one. In this stage of recovery she's also extremely sensitive and emotional. I'm helping her understand that someday she will have her beautiful and powerful singing voice back with practice. I secretly hope I'm right.

Beyond anything else, I have wanted Taylor's intense love and passion for music to come back to her. Today it has, and I am filled with joy. I'm grateful for that little gift today and that special five minutes we shared. I am grateful for Taylor taking this like a champ. She has been an excellent brain-injury patient lately, and I am proud of her. It's not an easy road.

Journal Entry Day 44
July 17th, 2014

Wooooosh...forty-four days? No wonder I'm so tired. Each day has felt like a month. I had a hard time falling asleep last night on the gym mat because of the sheer thrill pumping through my body from yesterday when Taylor mouthed the words to that song. That song that's obviously in her file cabinets of memory.

Today started out with Taylor sitting in a chair to eat, which is huge progress. She is normally in her wheelchair, tied in with a strap to hold her down. She's learning to not attempt an escape anymore. Then we had a visit from Dr. Kev, Taylor's orthodontist from home. We have not been able to get a proper and clear MRI because of the metal in her mouth. I asked him to come examine her and take her braces off in her hospital bed, if that could be possible. She did better than we expected, sitting still and understanding what was happening. Taylor is a favorite of his, and we were thrilled that he took the time to make this drive for her.

"Who wouldn't do this for Taylor?" he said to me.

I think Dr. Kev was also thrilled to see how well Taylor is

doing since hearing about her in the news. Dr. Kev got a lot of big smiles and three hugs from Taylor.

My sister, Lisa (my savior), arrived today and Taylor's exact words were, "Auntie Lisa, hiiiiiiii. Staci, Lisa Jenny, Laurel, Mita." And she kept repeating "Staci, Lisa, Jenny, Laurel, Mita," the order of my sisters, every time she looked at Lisa for two straight hours. "Staci, Lisa, Jenny, Laurel, Mita." Again, good to be able to find humor in it all.

We're working on Taylor's short-term memory because that's where a lot of the damage was done. Speech therapy is challenging to her right now because she says, "Um, I dunno," a lot.

Part of the struggle is she really *wants* to know the answers, but doesn't know things that she's sure she knew before. It's weird; it's almost like she remembers everything before that car hit her, and has a hard time remembering anything after it. We talked about the car a lot, and she told Christine today that she was "hit by a turkey, no wait, a turtle."

So it's part funny and part disturbing, but we know the kooky is all part of it. This morning Taylor asked me, "What does my schedule look like at the office today?"

And this personal assistant went right along with it. We're writing things down in a daily memory book, and we have lists and a calendar to help get her back on track. It may take a while but she's giving it all she's got. Oh, and apparently she has an office here? Good to know.

Later in the day it was emotional for me when Taylor asked many times about going home. She can tell you every single thing she misses, which would make any parent well up with tears. During therapy, Jenn saw a moment of clarity come over her and asked Taylor, "What are you thinking about?"

"I'm thinking about school...and what's gonna happen when I walk through those doors...and will I be able to read stuff," Taylor replied.

Lots of tears came after that, and Jenn has become a true friend. A therapist in more ways than one. Lots of goals have been set and one recently added is getting to Jenn's wedding in Hawaii come March. When Jenn invited us today, Taylor's jaw dropped open. "I wanna go!" was Taylor's response to that invite! Wouldn't it be great if we could make that trip?

A nurse used the term 'warp speed' regarding Taylor's progress these last few days. It's a roller coaster ride with many speeds and many changes. Sometimes it moves at an uneasy snail's pace for me, and as Emma said to me the other night while we were playing a game, "Patience, young Jedi, patience." Yes Emma, thank you.

I am holding patience more and more these days for Taylor, and for myself. These have been the toughest forty-four days of my life. Thank you all for wrapping your arms around me. I'm grabbing on tightly for this part of the ride.

Journal Entry Day 47
July 20th, 2014

Yesterday, Emma and I came to visit Taylor with a few of their cousins. Taylor has changed quite a bit since Emma saw her last week. There was a feeling of relief that came over Emma last night at bedtime. Voicing how the worst of this might be over, behind us, and each day is bringing Taylor closer to home. A wonderful conversation to be having.

Taylor received a special musical visit from Nate, her guitar teacher, today. Taylor's been asking for Nate, and we were excited to see him. To hear the sound of his guitar fill up this room, was comforting to both of us. I think the only thing missing was Taylor playing guitar with him. Someday soon, Taylor, I just know it. Taylor and Nate started by singing "I'll Fly Away" by Alan Jackson and the sweetest sound was hearing Taylor sing for the first time again with all her might. It was a beautiful sound. It used to bother her that her tone isn't quite there, but today she sang out. Nate and I loved it. She even proclaimed a "hallelujah" when they finished, hands in the air and all. Thank you, Nate. We sure do love you.

Taylor's still asking for her release date, and she asked the doctor today, "Are you working on my release date?"

His response to Taylor was, "You should come to our doctors' meeting and ask yourself."

Taylor replied without hesitation, "Okay, I will!"

No doubt she will. I still crack up when telling people how she thinks she's incarcerated with her release date to be decided, and not a discharge date.

When we speak about home there are still lots of tears. She said, "Please take me in your car, and we'll go home. It's easy."

Tears from me as well as her. I wish it were that easy. Taylor asked if she could visit home today and then come back here. I explained to her that when I take her home, she's staying there, and we're only coming back *here* to visit. No visits home, it's home you will stay my gorgeous girl. Possibly in a protective space suit if I get my way, but you'll be home.

Journal Entry Day 55
July 28th, 2014

Taylor had her first car ride and two big doctor appointments in Los Angeles at Kaiser, where she was first transferred to the ICU: first neurology and then her pelvic x-ray.

On our way from one appointment to the other, Taylor was in a wheelchair and a doctor stopped us on the sidewalk. He said he recognized Taylor by the school t-shirt she was wearing and introduced himself. That's when I recognized him as the surgeon who put Taylor's mic-key button in. He had seen Taylor a couple of times, and both of those times she was barely awake, not moving, and not talking. I could tell he was absolutely thrilled to see her, shake her hand, and especially thrilled to hear her talk to him.

After saying goodbye to us, he turned back to Taylor and said, "Hey, you know what? You just made my day!"

I began to cry while I hugged him goodbye because hearing him say that, made mine.

Second appointment was in orthopedics again with a doctor who first saw Taylor when she arrived in the ICU, and he was also thrilled to see her progress. Taylor was cleared to walk today. Pelvic and foot fractures are all healed. Yes, yes, and thank you.

Taylor was tired driving back in the car but still wanted to hit Islands restaurant near the hospital before we went back. It's tricky to know how much of the world she can take right now, but she also wanted to make three other stops, which started to sound more like an escape plan, so Islands was all we did. It didn't go so well; there was way too much stimulation, but maybe we'll get to a restaurant again someday.

We got back to HealthBridge in time to see Jenn and start walking. She started with a walker and that lasted for seconds. Once she found her balance, she took off down the hall on her own. Taylor is thrilled, and I know it makes Jenn happy as well. This is a real game changer for Taylor and managing our days here. Awesome to watch and what a relief. Note: If you see her coming down the hallway, beware of the wobbly walking Taylor.

Huge progress today. Taylor went for a ride in the car for the first time. First meal in a restaurant after all this time was huge too, even though we had some challenges. The most amazing part is that a week ago she could not have ridden in the car and made it through this big day. Every single day she is improving, and every single day after this one she will continue to work hard, and get herself back together. She's starting to understand what all of that means, which is great but also frustrating, because that also means the real work has only begun.

On the other side of this, it's so great to watch Taylor parade the halls while she's walking, smiling, and waving to everyone. That's our Taylor, no matter where she is, or what condition she's in, she's still smiling and lovely to everyone around her. The mayor if you will.

Jenn told her today in the hallway while we were resting that she has over 20,000 thousand people who have read this journal. Taylor's jaw dropped and stayed there awhile. She used to bribe Emma for likes on Instagram to hit 100. So she knows exactly what that means.

Taylor and I went back to her room and had a nice chat about how many people love us, love her, and how many hands are holding ours right now. I hope she takes many good things away from this journey, but most importantly, I hope she feels, understands, and recognizes the love that surrounds her. Love that will last forever. Tonight we pulled out this journal and started reading it together. She wants to know, and she really wants to understand. Interesting to go back to my first entries.

Journal Entry Day 56
July 29th, 2014

Taylor went to bed early last night and woke up late this morning: obviously exhausted from our big day. She did a lot of walking today, and with that will come learning to take care of herself again. Occupational therapy is working with her on things like brushing teeth (which includes putting the cap back on the toothpaste) and even cleaning up after yourself. Now if those two things stick, that might actually be the first bonus for me.

Taylor's doing great in speech therapy, and they're working on switching from one thing to another. I am watching closely, and comparing what she can do now to what she couldn't do a week ago is amazing! She's still bothered by the way her voice sounds and its new tone. She still lacks fluctuation, and her sound is monotone. Hearing tests to come. She is still concerned about her singing voice and when that will come back, but I keep assuring her it will.

Swimming was on the board for 1 pm and Taylor was so excited. I think the idea of going to the pool with her three favorite therapists is more fun for Taylor than anything. I'm quite sure she'd rather go to Sephora with them, but a pool workout will suffice. Sephora someday in the future. Running in place, jumping jacks, a few laps, and a lot of laughs make for a good therapy day.

The countdown begins, and when Taylor wakes up tomorrow morning she will ask and then repeat several times that she has NINE days left at HealthBridge. August 8th will be her release date. It was confirmed in our family meeting today that August 8th is in fact her discharge date. August 8th, and don't forget.

Taylor still wants it changed to sooner, and Dory still asks all day long, "How many days left?"

A nurse heard her in the hallway say, "Mom, if they don't let me out on that exact day, you'll help me with that escape plan we talked about, right?" Laughs all around.

On one of our walks today she tried to get me to put her in the car and take her home quickly. She goes back and forth on completely understanding why we're here. I know how much she misses home because I know how much I miss having her there. I told Dory again that we need her to come home and be able to safely do things on her own.

Jenn has made sure that they switch her therapies tomorrow to acute rehab, and we explained to Taylor that for the next eight days, she's going to do some serious work to get strong. One day for packing, the other days to get strong. She really can't wait to pack.

The greatest moment today was when Taylor and I took a walk outside after dinner and she had her arm around me. I noticed how long it has been since we've done that, and I started to get emotional. I also noticed she got taller.

We were talking and laughing about funny things that happened today, and it made me pause for a moment. I love her to pieces. At one point I looked at her face as she was talking to me and let it all sink in. Holding tears back the best I could. She is *walking*, and she is *talking*, and she's laughing. Not only have I been waiting for this moment for a long time, but I also wondered if it would ever happen. It has happened! Even though it's been fifty-six grueling days, I am grateful for tonight's little stroll in the park. Taylor is evidence of a miracle. I truly believe that.

Journal Entry Day 59
August 1st, 2014

Taylor's last Friday in the hospital. She knows it's her last Friday, and she knows she's going home on August 8th, but she still keeps forgetting. And sometimes when you re-tell her, it's like she's hearing it for the first time, so she celebrates, tears and all. These Dory visits, and her short-term memory, are a real struggle. But we power through.

Taylor got her mic-key button taken out this morning since she's recently been taking everything by mouth, which has been used as incentive to get to go home. She was overjoyed to say goodbye to that feeding tube, and the hole in her stomach is a lot like a second little belly button. Taylor said, regarding the hole, "It's better than having the tube!"

We had a great day, and occupational therapists are working on things like making her bed, morning routine, getting dressed, and doing sort of a dress rehearsal for a day at home. Having no short-term memory is difficult for everyone involved, and being prepared for that is really important. Emma is really going to have to help assist Dory when we get home because I need a break.

Physical therapy was a workout today, and she was out of breath when we got back, which is good. Taylor is getting stronger and she likes that feeling. We're practicing things like walking backwards and keeping your balance, walking on plank boards slowly, and walking up ramps, walking in grass, jumping, and landing. What's amazing is watching her body at fourteen relearn things that she learned when she was a munchkin. It's all fascinating to me. We had an afternoon full of games (mostly memory), and Taylor is shocking me with how good she is at it. She wants to be quizzed at math, and she wants to be fed information and asked questions to test her memory. She wants to remember everything and fast. The pace isn't fast at all, which is the hard part for her.

We were eating dinner outside tonight, and saw Brian, the CEO of HealthBridge Hospital. He asked me if Taylor has always been this happy and polite. I looked at him, smiled, and said, "Yes, Brian. Yes she has, and I'm thrilled it stuck."

These last two months have been the hardest Taylor will ever experience in her life (hopefully), and yet she never wavered from her kind and happy spirit, *ever*. Whatever the future brings, Taylor will still continue to have that smile on her face. These days are long in the hospital, and my days at home are hard because I'm not at the hospital. There is also a whole other side of this ordeal, which is dealing with insurance, doctors, bills, where we're going next, more bills, what the future looks like, and all the other details. It's hard, it's tiring, and it's the most difficult work I've ever done by far. When I see that smile on Taylor's face, it makes it all worth it. Even after repeating her release date to her for the nine-hundredth time today. Until I write again, friends. Until then...

Journal Entry Day 60
August 2nd, 2014

Two months in a hospital! Taylor knows it and she is *way* over it. She woke up at 4:30 this morning and every five seconds was asking when she was going home, how many days was that, and will I break her out if they don't let her go, etc., etc. I needed some more sleep, so I wheeled her down to the nurses for an hour so she could question them. When she came back to me I quickly got a big Sharpie marker and wrote on the back of her hands:

FRIDAY, AUGUST 8TH
6 DAYS

Each day that number will change, and each day I will write it for her because it worked and now she knows where she can look to get the answer.

We had a busy day with all her therapies and a massage in between. I had to sneak our masseuse, Sharon, in as a friend, which she is, but the hospital technically can't know she's here to work on Taylor. After her massage, Taylor said, "My voice sounds different."

And it was true. I can't wait for all sorts of massage, yoga, and acupuncture that's close to home to help her get better.

Physical therapy was last, and they decided to take Taylor on a little walk to the corner store to buy something. We had to cross one street for the first time together, and a strange feeling came over me. I couldn't help thinking what that moment of the car hitting her was like, since this is the first time she's been in a crosswalk. Suddenly that little street we were crossing felt endlessly long, but she did it. Once we got to the little store the therapists gave her instructions, and Taylor headed straight to the candy aisle to buy her first treats. I gave her money and she did everything herself. We quizzed her on change and she did great. Honestly she looks like she's a few cocktails in when she walks, but that will all straighten out eventually. After all, it's only been five days since she started walking.

Tonight we were able to FaceTime Taylor's bluegrass band from her summer camp while they played their last concert. They all gave Taylor a big shout-out, which she loved. I know Taylor really wanted to be there tonight singing her heart out and playing that guitar. I know she misses it.

I gazed at her with admiration while she watched her fellow students, with a giant smile on her face, and I had a little prideful cry. She comforted me by putting her arm around me as we continued to watch. She has the best attitude. I wish she could have been there and not here. But I wish a lot for her right now, and next year it will all be different. I promised her that much.

Oh, and in case you didn't know (or you forgot), August 8th is the day; it's a Friday coming soon, and there are six days left. Six days. August 8th. Do ya think Rain Man is rubbing off on me a little?

Journal Entry Day 63
August 5th, 2014

Today went quickly, thank goodness, because if Taylor isn't distracted, the question is asked every ten seconds. Even though it's written in Sharpie marker everywhere on her body and in her room at this point. She even joined us in the family meeting with the doctors today to ask them some questions. No fear at all. We found out she still is in fact going home on Friday, August 8th. Three days from now, and the countdown begins.

Three, two and then one! I'm even starting to count the hours.

Another day of swimming with our favorite therapists and

learning things from Jenn that we can do for some home therapy. I'm learning a lot in therapy sessions now since a lot of the therapy she gets at home will be coming from us. There are moments in the day when I can't believe Taylor has to literally relearn everything. Everything she knows, and everything she has ever done. She'll catch on, but new tasks require a certain review process that's fairly time-consuming right now.

Taylor took a shot at handwriting today for the first time, and it quickly became painfully frustrating for her. She pushed it away and gave herself a moment. I saw the tears start, and I know this is all a struggle for her. It pains me to watch, so I can't even imagine how it feels. She's working on embracing that challenging right hand. Her brain knows what it should do, but the function isn't there yet. We've been told the frustration for her may get worse as she realizes her limitations. That will most likely be when we're home. I'm looking forward to the transition, but I also am well aware of how challenging it will be. Taylor wants to feel normal in her body and she doesn't. It's tricky when you're in the hospital around other injured or sick children, and Taylor is improving, but when we go home I sense the change will be daunting to her. The pace of home, things she used to do at home that won't come easy to her right away. At home she will no longer be the star patient either. I just hope that we will all be able to comfort Taylor in some way as the reality of this whole situation and her world as we know it starts to sink in. I know it won't be easy.

This evening was filled with giant laughs for a lot of us. Our favorite nurse, Fred, was a really good sport and let Taylor put some makeup and jewelry on him. She laughed so hard and then asked if she could parade him around the hallway to show everyone. Who could say no to that? It was great. It was hilarious, and I will really miss this place and these great people.

Lots of tears at bedtime tonight because when fatigue sets in, everything appears jumbled and confusing to Taylor. If this is all hard for *me* to sort out sometimes, I can't imagine what it's like for her. I now understand how important rest and sleep are for our brains.

Hang in there Taylor, and stay strong.

Journal Entry Day 64
August 6th, 2014

I sit in a chair next to Taylor in this room and I can only think of how she was when we first arrived. I was reminded of her first day a lot today as I said goodbye to some of the staff who are now some beautiful friends we've made here. I hugged them goodbye with deep appreciation for what they do, and who they have been to Taylor. There were a lot of tears, but mostly with a grateful heart for all of them. I'm writing my last journal entry from room number one: reminded of the day we got to move in because the girl who was in it before us, went home. I was thrilled for her, and now I feel over the moon for Taylor; she's going home.

All of these people who saw Taylor when she first arrived know how far she's come, and they have all been a part of her incredible progress. They have also been captured by Taylor's spirit and are elated to see her preparing to go home. Some have mentioned that keeping the Little Mayor here forever might be nice, but they know she'll be having none of that.

The hardest goodbye for Taylor will be to Jenn because we had to say goodbye to her today. Jenn won't be here on discharge/release day. I knew from the moment Taylor laid eyes on Jenn they would be instant friends. We will see Jenn someday soon, and it won't be here.

Taylor is sleeping through the night now, and when she wakes in the morning she will have one more day in a hospital. I know she'll be repeating that all day long, and I won't mind at all.

As much as Taylor's felt like she's been doing time in pris-
on, I've been sharing stories with her of what she was like
when all these people first met her. Taylor knows she's gotten
better here, doesn't remember ninety-nine percent of it, and
doesn't really understand how much better she got.

When someone in Taylor's condition gets this close to going
home, they can't understand why they have to wait, which has
made these last few days quite grueling. Every time we've been
outside she says that she prays that one time we'll be locked
out of the hospital so we can escape and run to the car. She's
been super consistent with that and also forgetting every time
that the key to the car is inside the hospital. We've talked about
going home constantly, and it's been difficult for her to focus
on anything else. When we get her home she knows what's
coming her way: a lot of work, a lot of doctor appointments,
and more work. She's up for it and at this point only wants to
be home. I completely understand.

Friday morning, August 8th will be a wonderful day indeed.
It will be sixty-six days in the hospital with her. It has been a
journey and one that is not over, but one that is taking a sharp
turn.

CHAPTER 11

Coming Home

It was a Friday. Taylor was being discharged from Health-Bridge Children's Hospital in Orange County. Mike had spent the night with Taylor, while I had been at home getting Emma ready for her first five-night sleepover camp. Emma was going to camp with her best friend in order to buy us some time. She hadn't seen much of Taylor yet, so it was important to get Taylor re-acclimated at home first, and then Emma would return two nights later. I was systematically (and manically) getting the house in order for Taylor.

Mike and I had agreed that Taylor would spend her first week or two at my house. On the practical side, my house was easier because we could pull the car into the driveway and get really close to the front door. I knew I would be showering with her, helping her get dressed, and all the other things. We hoped that by the time she went to her dad's house, she would be managing much of the self-care thing on her own, needing only a little assistance.

The labeling, cleaning, and simplifying that I had been doing nonstop for three days came easy to me. This time it wasn't so much driven by my obsession with order as much as my clear knowledge that an organized and clutter-free world is key for a brain injury and the anxiety that comes with it.

At 7 am the house was in order, and Emma had already been at camp in Big Bear for three nights. I was getting a ride to the hospital that morning so Mike, Taylor, and I could all drive home together in his car. Traveling with Taylor in the car required one person to be on Taylor duty in the seat next to her while one person drove. I was going to be on Taylor duty in the back seat.

During my hour ride down there for discharge day, I had thought about what the long car ride home with Taylor would be like. I was hoping this drive would be different from the previous two we had with her going to Los Angeles for doctor appointments. Taylor had unbuckled her seatbelt on one of the rides because she was frustrated and not feeling well sitting in traffic. She was desperate to get out of the car and thought she could at forty miles an hour on the freeway. She got carsick quickly, and claustrophobia came over her, which made her panic while she was throwing up. The first time this happened, we were not prepared. The good news was I learned quickly and had a stash of plastic bags and wipes in my bag. I was reviewing every scenario that happened before, and I was going through the checklist of things that could happen. I hoped it would go smoothly because the destination was home. She hadn't been there in sixty-six days!

When I started to see HealthBridge's entrance from afar I smirked as I stared at the front porch—the front porch where Taylor and I had sat many mornings talking about her escape or breaking out of there. HealthBridge is the most un-hospital looking building. It was a happy yellow house with a front porch that had a dozen big white wooden rocking chairs sprinkled all over it. Taylor and I had spent a lot of time out there when she could go outside between therapies. Now, Taylor was actually coming home. I put my head in my hands and began to cry.

As the car pulled into the entrance circle, I was a color wheel of different emotions: excited that we had made it to this moment, terrified out of my mind, and grateful that she proved so many doctors wrong, and elated that Taylor was coming home, not in a wheelchair, not with a walker, but on her own two feet. I felt fortunate at the same time that I was extremely aware of two other families at HealthBridge. Their children were not walking or talking and, sadly, might not again. My daughter was finally coming home.

Taylor was ready. We were ready. And whatever came next, we would conquer it. In the front doors I went, for that last walk down those hospital halls to her room. Suddenly, I felt strong and extremely focused. I opened the door to her room, and there they were. What a sight! Taylor was sitting on the edge of her bed and Mike was tying her shoes.

"Taylor, it's August 8th!" I said.

She gave me the biggest brightest smile. "Mom, let's goooooo. Now!" Though Taylor was clearly ready, we had to wait for the discharge papers and medication instructions. In other words, it was forty-five minutes of Taylor constantly pleading. "Why can't we go? When can we leave? I wanna go home."

Then the nurse walked in with the papers and told us that Taylor was cleared by the doctor to leave the hospital.

HealthBridge has a special ritual they do for patients on discharge day. "Rainbow in five minutes! Rainbow in five minutes!" was announced over the loudspeaker. Doctors, nurses, patients, and visitors lined the big hallway that led to the exit, ready to celebrate the patient who was fortunate enough to leave. The three of us stood in her room for the last time, holding each other. Then off Taylor went, exiting room number one for the last time, and we proudly followed.

I hadn't seen that many people in the hallway before. There were balloons, gifts, signs, and kids in wheelchairs cheering her on. Every single nurse who was ever assigned to her hugged and congratulated her, therapists too. Even the director of the hospital was emotional. I had planned to add my own celebration to this moment. I had a speaker in my bag and it was blasting "Just the Way You Are" by Bru-no Mars as Taylor walked alone for the first time down that hallway. Until then she had always been required to wear a safety belt tied around her waist. Taylor was walking proud and absolutely beaming. A little wobbly, but standing proud!

I tried to sing along in between my tears, and at one point Amy, her nurse for many days, and I belted out part of the chorus. I felt so much love from those people who had worked so hard and had never once disappointed us. Taylor was taking the time to say goodbye to everyone in the corri-dor and on the porch. This was the old Taylor, the baby who greeted everyone on our walks, the girl who always spoke to parents and adults at her school. Now she was standing on that same porch where we had eaten breakfast almost every day and joked about me putting her in the car when they weren't looking. There we were saying our goodbyes. What a sight. We took some photos and assured everyone we would be back in a few months, "But only to visit," Taylor kept say-ing. "Only to visit, right mom?"

"Yes, Taylor—only to visit."

I can still remember that moment when I stopped to watch Taylor walk out of that hospital on August 8th, the place that had become a second womb, that had rebirthed her in a way. Our bridge to home. I was thrilled for her and all of us.

We got into Mike's van and waved goodbye to all our new friends. The three of us were alone in the car leaving that place that had most definitely fulfilled its mission statement for us. We were all quiet, and I suddenly remembered the day we had left the hospital with Taylor as an infant in the bucket seat. I had felt complete, the baby out of my body, my job as a mom finally beginning. I had felt so much love for that baby girl. That same feeling enveloped me now. Here we were to-gether, though with many differences. Mike and I were no longer a couple, and though Taylor was not a baby, she was in many ways like one. She had a lot to learn and do as she re-entered this real world. A big part of her journey was still ahead of us.

"Let's go home..." I said, once again, sure that we would conquer any obstacle.

"Yeah. I can't wait. Let's go home. Let's go home. Let's go home," Taylor chanted.

Journal Entry Day 66
August 8th, 2014

What a day to remember. I'm told that it's not often (never, by some people here) that a child has physically walked out of HealthBridge Children's Hospital. How lucky we were today. I cried tears of overwhelming gratitude for this moment and each and every one of our friends here at HealthBridge. Taylor was thrilled to be breaking out, and what a beautiful sight it was to see her open the door to her room, and walk toward the front hallway, to hear the excitement, the clapping, and the cheering. That is where she paused and stood up a little straighter. I remember smiling at that.

Down the front hallway she went. As she headed toward the front door, she was hugging all the supportive and loving teary-eyed staff. Tears of joy from everyone, and as the front desk girl said, "...It was a *very* special goodbye. One like no other."

Thank you HealthBridge Children's Hospital. We love each and every one of you, and we will never, ever forget you. After all, in what other hospital can you plan a flash mob during lunch? Just sayin'...you rock!

We are home, we are safe, and this mama couldn't be happier. A new chapter begins, and this one will be from home. I will continue to journal, and I hope you all will continue to read and write back. It is my therapy, it is my comfort, and it is where

I feel most connected and supported by all of you right now. Hopefully, we'll even get to see some of you!

Taylor and I had a nice quiet dinner, and she's spending time getting comfortable being home again. She'll be here for a bit with me and then venture on to Dad's house. Mike and I are a team during this no matter what. Emma comes home from camp tomorrow, and Taylor is anxious to see her. Hopefully Emma will find some balance in us being together again. The new questions from Dory:

"When will my voice be the same? When will my eye look the same?"

I answer by saying that's what we're home to do: work hard and make it all the same.

Friday, August 8th, Taylor is home. Remarkable really and I will continue to hold onto my faith and keep believing. So will Taylor.

CHAPTER 12

Our New Normal

We were finally home. As we pulled into the driveway, we noticed beach balls everywhere, palm trees and swim floats, and all things summery in my front yard. There was even a big *Welcome Home Taylor* sign too. Taylor had been speaking to Maggie, our friend who grew up across the street from my girls, throughout her hospital stay. Taylor had expressed how bummed she was that she had missed out on her whole summer. Well, Maggie took care of that and certainly made Taylor feel like she still had some summer left. Taylor loved the summer décor sprinkled in the front yard, and I don't think she stopped smiling for a full hour.

Watching Taylor navigate around the house was interesting at first. She began reacquainting herself with her own room, the kitchen, and where her things were. I felt strange, and it was unnerving to leave her in her room alone after so long. It was hard wired in my brain after sixty-six days in a hospital room to never leave her alone. Her escape tactics still had me on high alert, but I had to keep reminding myself that her goal was to get *here*. It was hard for me to forget that Taylor had only recently started walking. Her balance was still off, and even though she would walk slowly, anything could happen, so letting her wander freely around the house was not easy for me. I knew I had to give her some space and let Taylor at least begin to feel independent again. Meanwhile, the only thing I wanted was for her to wear a helmet, and she was having none of that.

101

The first few nights were especially nerve-racking, but I thought it was important that she sleep in her own bed and learn how to be home again. Taylor slept like a rock, and I didn't. I felt so far away being in separate rooms now, and I kept wondering if she woke up, would I hear her, and if she needed something, would she try to get up and get it? Would she find it or would she have a crazy episode? Would she know where she was? A lot of questions were running through my head, and I was always preparing for different middle-of-the-night scenarios, or daytime ones as well. There was no big, red-call-button to push anymore for help. It was only me, by myself, with her.

Emma came home from camp after two nights of Taylor and I being alone in the house. When they first saw each other, it was such an interesting moment. It was like we were back to normal, yet we all knew we weren't. We very much weren't. Emma didn't really know what to say to Taylor or how to react to her. Emma spent a lot of those first few hours observing her. The whole scenario would be difficult for any-one, and Emma was twelve looking at her big sister who was acting like a five-year-old.

It was the fifth morning of being home when Taylor found out that her ninth grade-class was going on an orientation weekend away. She quickly figured out that she would not be included in that trip, and she went berserk as she was telling me. Apparently, Taylor heard this news from a classmate via text—and I wanted to drop-kick that girl. Taylor became irate with *me* suddenly, and I knew I had to think quickly as she exploded within ten seconds of telling me. That's when my defenses went up.

With a brain injury, the filter that most of us have com-pletely disappears at times for the injured. That especially happens when there are emotions involved. Also, the more upset and agitated the brain gets, the more it can't calm down. When this agitation is heightened, it takes time and some kind of big distraction to snap them out of it. While these episodes are happening, they can be scary and disturbing to the witnesses, and sometimes violent.

Taylor said awful things to me and looked like she was on fire by the way she was moving around and talking crazy. She started to head out the door as she was screaming, "I'm going on that trip!" and then it really started. As I saw Taylor bolt for the door I was able to act quickly because even though Taylor was pissed off, her reflexes were still lagging and she was still wobbly in her balance. So bolting for Taylor looked like she was in slow motion compared to me. I grabbed her and had to bend her legs with my leg in order to wrestle her to the ground. I knew that if she opened that door, she was going to run as fast as she could and become completely disoriented. I thought the worst: that she would run into the street, in front of a car.

I was able to get on top of her and spoke calmly to her. I let her know that she was losing control and she had to dial it back, but it was clear to me that she couldn't. I was straddling her body, and holding her arms down when Taylor started kicking and fighting for her life. Emma was watching all of it from the corner of the living room, and when I saw her I said, "Em, I need you to call your Dad right now. If he doesn't answer, you need to dial 911."

Emma called her dad, and thankfully Mike answered. I only hoped I would be able to restrain Taylor by myself until he got there. He arrived in seven minutes, and then both of us could muscle her. For forty-five more minutes, Taylor tried to bolt out the door. It was a complete battle of reasoning with her while she was physically putting up a good fight too. After Taylor finally came out of that tough 'brain-storm,' she understood why she could not go with her classmates. Mike and I were exhausted.

Her dad left, and I got Taylor settled in front of the TV for an hour-long show. I sat with her for a few minutes and then had to make my way into my bedroom, shut the door, and quietly weep in my hands. That whole scene broke my heart. Watching your child be so out of control is extremely difficult.

When Taylor was able to reflect on that scene, remember her rage, and connect with it, I tearfully explained to her that if she continued to do that and act out physically, she wouldn't be able to stay at home anymore. She would have to go back to the hospital if she couldn't learn to restrain herself. Thankfully, Taylor wanted none of that, so every time I would see things start to escalate from then on, I had to give her the hospital warning, which worked like magic.

Taylor acting out physically was the most difficult thing for a while. She would throw punches or grab things that were on the table and throw them at us. We made a deal that when I saw her start to get frustrated inside herself, she would have to go into her room and take a five-minute time-out. Luckily for us, her long-term memory knew exactly what a time-out was, and it worked like a charm.

Not being able to do things like she used to, was becoming extremely frustrating for Taylor, and these outbursts were happening more frequently at home. Therapists explained that her limitations, as she was slowly coming back into her brain and body, would become challenging in more ways than one. Taylor was also remembering more about her old self while everything felt different to her. The things that she used to be able to do on her own had completely changed. Showering by herself, washing her hair, tying her own shoes… so many little things. And now, her friends, who she hadn't seen in months, were all going on an orientation trip that she remembered hearing about in the last weeks of school. She wouldn't be starting school with them, and those friends were also not calling or texting her. Everything had changed. Taylor knew it, was aware of it, and felt no control over any of it.

Going out into the world on occasion also became interesting. Things like going into the grocery store, having a meal in a restaurant, or small gatherings with friends or family. I would often gauge Taylor's daily function by how many imaginary martinis she'd had that morning. This way people could have a good idea of what we were dealing with in terms of brain function. Not real martinis of course, but it was a good measure to give people, so they could understand why she would be acting the way she was. It was also a way for me to keep it light and humorous.

There were days when Taylor was much more on point than others, and other days were just hard. The difficult ones were when she would throw up within five minutes of being in the car or sometimes seem more disoriented in her surroundings. Some days she would forget the things she needed to bring with her or just leave them behind in random places. There were days when the names of people would totally escape her. It would depend on the day, and there was no understanding of why. There were good days and horrible days for her functionality and memory. I had the martini rating system for only close friends who were around her often. The martinis became helpful as an understanding (or comparison) of having a slightly buzzed or fully drunk girlfriend with you. If she was three or four martinis in, she would need more help navigating through the day. Taylor was a fun buzzed or drunk girlfriend to have with you, but there were some days when I felt like ditching her. Some days when I was in overload and my patience was wearing thin, it got to be too much. Those were difficult days because of the sheer emotional exhaustion of it, but also the guilt I felt sometimes of not wanting to be with her. Then the thought, *I could use a couple martinis right about now,* would creep in. Kind of like, if you can't beat 'em, join 'em; but that wasn't who I was, and my focus had to be laser sharp.

It is still mind-boggling to me how one day Taylor could be one martini in, and the next she could be a wasted drunk girl all day long: not able to walk straight, falling down, losing things, not speaking clearly, losing thoughts, and asking the same thing over and over again. Hard to be with and hard to watch, but I always knew she would sober up at some point. And patience was the key. I still rate Taylor on martinis, but on a much different scale.

Taylor being home got a lot easier after the first couple of weeks. At night, it was difficult for me to listen to her night terrors. She would talk in her sleep, and only jumbles of words would come out, which would freak me out. I didn't sleep through the night for three months after Taylor came home, much like when she was an infant.

It was at the end of November 2014 when Taylor was standing over me while I was sleeping. I sensed her there, and she scared the living daylights out of me when I actually saw her. She was at the side of my bed like a statue, and it took her a while to respond to my asking her if she was okay.

She finally said, "Mom, I saw the car. It was coming toward me."

My heart sank, and I tried to console her and explain that these visions might be helpful to her but also a little scary. I let her get into my bed and assured her that, as scary as that was, she had nothing to be afraid of. She was safe now. We were on our own now as these things would start to happen, and we would have to deal with all of them.

Our new normal became moments of complete chaos with a drunk Taylor, to moments of great sweetness. When Emma and Taylor were together and not fighting there were precious times of Emma taking on the role of big sis. I know it wasn't easy for Emma to feel so needed, but Taylor didn't remember how to do certain things like work the remote on the TV, bounce a basketball, or play games that we used to play. So Emma, who has the patience of a saint, would sit and reteach her. There was one morning when I came around a corner and saw Taylor with her eye patch on, sitting on the floor with Emma who was showing Taylor how to set up the Zhu Zhu Pet track. They hadn't pulled that out for seven years, and there they both were going back in time to their childhood together.

It was hard for all of us to accept our new roles when Taylor came home. It was difficult having to navigate our moods around Taylor most days, as she would generally set the tone, and we would all fall in line. The hardest part for me was physically seeing her in our house like normal, but yet she was so different. The thought of having to grieve the old Taylor was heavy on my mind and always at the forefront. I knew I had to embrace the new Taylor in front of me, and I knew I had to be gentle with myself (and her) in the process.

Journal Entry Day 67
August 9th, 2014

I knew it would be easier in some ways to be home, but I also knew it would be hard. Taylor has more distractions here, which is good, but it is here that she is much more aware of feeling and being different.

She had her first of many acupuncture appointments today, and she did really great. She is staying open-minded and is willing to embrace new things to get better. With four needles in her head, four around her eye, some down her entire body, and one in each toe, Taylor took it like a champ.

Emma got home from camp and it was great to have both girls together again. Mike and I loved seeing them be so comforting and soft toward one another. Truly special. I can also

tell that Emma is going to be a huge help to me. She always has
been, but this is different. Emma has moved into the big sister
role now. She is being patient with helping Taylor get familiar
with things again. Emma is a pretty special twelve-year-old,
and it's all beautiful to watch. We're all setting our rhythm to
Taylor's for now and it looks to be working, which is great. We
will push her, but also let her take the lead in some aspects.

Taylor said a few things to me tonight at bedtime that stuck
out:

"Mom, I miss you, and I miss being myself."

The other was, "Mom, I love you, and you're so awesome."
With that being said, I'm good for as long as this takes.

Journal Entry Day 70
August 12th, 2014

These have been extremely busy days. Emma is the proud
owner of a new betta fish. She's had to wait a long time since
the first week of the accident when Puddles...well, it got too
hot in the house for poor Puddles. Emma's happy and Blizzard
looks to be that way too.

Taylor was evaluated at the Center for Neuro Skills (CNS)
on Monday morning for three hours, and we found out she
is in fact a candidate for their wonderful program. We were
hoping for that, so she could start as soon as possible. CNS will
hopefully be a part of our routine as early as next week, which
is excellent news.

Taylor was also fortunate to get in to see Dr. Bose this
morning for another three hours at Cedars Sinai. He is a neu-
ro-ophthalmologist and not only is he a wonderful doctor, but
he is also a wonderful human. Dr. Bose is Indian, speaks En-
glish with a thick accent, and everything about him is lovely.
I couldn't take my eyes off of him when he spoke. He asked
Taylor things like, "Taylor, how do you feel? What bothers you?

What are your wishes? ...Please tell me."

I tell you, he is amazing!

Dr. Bose also said, "Taylor, I see from my testing that your optic nerve and retina are intact, and they look so very beautiful to me."

Taylor's smile sent Mike and I both into tears. That is also the exact news we were looking to hear. Much more from Dr. Bose sent me into tears, as he explained to Taylor that he sees people like her every day because of accidents and other things, and she can overcome this. It will take some hard work, but she will overcome it, and she has youth on her side. He also mentioned not losing focus and keeping a positive attitude, which will always be important for Taylor to hear. The sum of it all is, Taylor's eye could get better with a lot of therapy ahead. There is some nerve damage, which may never heal, but there is no severe damage to the inside of her eye. We go back for special glasses on Wednesday to start this whole process.

Taylor has asked me many times this afternoon what street she was walking on when she was hit. She doesn't understand what crosswalk she was in when I try to explain to her, so this afternoon she asked if we could drive by. I drove by the scene by myself a month ago for a different reason. I had to know why that driver didn't swerve left or right. Why did he choose to go straight? Well, I saw it. There was a concrete wall on the left and concrete on the right. I guess he had no choice, really.

We loaded up in the car, and Emma and I showed her. We started at the park and I showed her where she was walking, and then I pointed out where the car was coming from that hit them. Taylor said, "Ohhhhhhhhh," and then silence. Thirty seconds later she said, looking out the car window, "That stupid car. I wish that never happened."

Me too, Taylor, me too.

Journal Entry Day 74
August 16th, 2014

I was next to Taylor during her acupuncture treatment where we're working on circulation. Because it works, I have to sit next to her and help her with the areas that itch a lot. While she was lying there settling in, she turned to me (needles sticking out from everywhere in her face) with the most endearing and genuine, "Mom, how are you?"

I told her, "I'm good babe. Now you close your eyes and try to rest." All I could do after that was drop my head and sob quietly.

Oh how great it's been having Taylor home. But as you can imagine, it certainly has its challenges. Taylor wants to be herself again and she has moments when she thinks she is, which is the difficult part. Taylor and Emma will be going back and forth between two houses now, with both Mike and I involved in what Taylor does and her schedule.

We found out late yesterday that Taylor will be starting at CNS on Monday morning. She will go there five days a week, five hours a day with a one-hour lunch break. Much like school but it's more work for Taylor than anything else.

It's hard for her to comprehend how much work that really is, but she has three wishes:

To get her eye fixed

To go back to school

To get her singing voice back

I have vowed to make sure all of that has a chance to happen, and I'll do whatever I need to get those opportunities for her.

We know CNS is the place where Taylor needs to be right now, and where our health insurance wants to put her for rehab won't cut it. As many of you know, Taylor came from HealthBridge Hospital doing four hours a day of therapies.

Since being home, she has only gotten four hours a week, with Mike and I filling in the gaps.

After emails, phone calls, and seeing many of their doctors, our insurance still thinks that four hours a week of therapy will suffice. Mike and I both agree that's just not good enough. Taylor deserves the best, and she deserves the opportunity to be able to recover. CNS is the best, and they have everything Taylor needs at this point in her recovery. They are advanced, and they are cutting edge with specific therapies for her hand, her memory, her cognitive thinking, and all those important things that she wants back. They have a neuro-optometrist, and they also have psych therapy for Taylor and for our whole family as well. Dr. Bose knows CNS well and is a fan. CNS will also play a big role in transitioning Taylor back into school when the time comes. But for now, she has her own locker and her own schedule that she follows daily all by herself. We will be involved and there every day with her for the first few weeks, but then Mike and I will slowly disappear, being there for only the key things. Huge bonus for us, being that it's only five miles away.

CNS will cost us $1100.00 per day, and we won't know how long Taylor will need to be in their program, until they are able to assess her needs for at least two weeks. That number is daunting, in more ways than one, but I am determined to figure it out. Every weekday I touch base with the insurance company to keep them in the loop. I am both excited and scared to start these next big steps forward, but I will continue to remain mindful, patient, and grateful.

part
four

CHAPTER 13

Our Village

Juggling the days was not easy. Taylor's schedule was the priority, but I also had to make Emma and myself a priority. I had to start working again mostly for my own sanity, but also for money, health insurance, and to feel like I had a life outside of caring for Taylor.

Once Taylor started rehabilitation at CNS and I began working again, the schedule became crazy with pick-ups and drop-offs. I needed to call on friends a lot of the time for help. No one ever said no, and there was this village of people helping us and willing to be in charge of Taylor whenever needed. My friends acted like it was a privilege for them to drive Taylor or accompany her to an appointment, and we all would especially get a kick out of her on the three-martinis-in days. She was funny, forgetful, and quirky. Everyone was making the best of it, which was all we could do. No point in dwelling on how drunk she was and why; it was easier to laugh with one another.

On the business side, bills were piling up. So much so that I don't remember seeing the one for her ambulance that was now in collections. It was October, and four months had flown by. I really hadn't paid attention to any of those things, but in reality, it was time. I was asked to have breakfast with a couple of friends who had ninth graders in Taylor's class, both of whom have known Taylor since kindergarten. They suggested we do a fundraiser on a bigger level in order to help us pay the bills and sustain us for a while. That morning over breakfast it turned into a fundraising plan for us, and it was on the heels of the hugely popular ALS Ice Bucket Challenge. My friends Monica and Michon brilliantly suggested a Taylor Pie-Smash Challenge. You take a pie in the face, raise money, and then pass on the challenge to someone else. The fundraiser exploded throughout our community and raised over one hundred thousand dollars. That led to a star-studded night of talent, which raised over thirty thousand dollars. Aside from these fundraisers, our friends, family, and community separately raised one hundred and forty thousand dollars with people sending cards and checks to Taylor. Our school community was incredible. Being able to pay the bills that were building up and the outside therapists and doctors for Taylor was an enormous relief; and I am forever grateful to everyone who so generously gave. I had hoped to be able to start paying it forward at some point throughout this journey.

In early November, I got a call from Jim, a director at Northridge Hospital where Taylor was taken that first day to the trauma unit. Jim mentioned that he had spoken to a couple of employees at the hospital who had nominated me to speak that year at their annual Humankindness Gala on October 11th. Without any hesitation, I told Jim that I would be honored to tell our story and help raise money for a hospital that I had the utmost respect for. It was a no-brainer for me, but hard to believe it was just four months after 'that day.' Jim and I met that week at the hospital with a few other staff members and at the end of our meeting they said *they* would be honored to have me speak. What, really? I was touched and became a little emotional, accepted the invitation, and realized *that* was where my paying it forward would begin.

Journal Entry Day 144
October 12th, 2014

I was honored when the president of the Northridge Hospital Foundation asked me to speak at their Humankindness Gala last night. I told our story in front of five hundred people. It was difficult for me but beautifully received—especially when Taylor came on stage to say a few words to roaring applause. It was great. The best part was that Kim and Julie (her nurses from Northridge) and Dr. Kang sat at a table with us. It's been 135 days since they've all seen Taylor, and last night we all had a joyful, tear-filled reunion.

I've told Taylor many stories about her days at Northridge Hospital, and she was elated to finally meet her crew of heroes there. I know they were all absolutely thrilled to see her.

Last weekend we had a visit from Jenn, Taylor's awesome physical therapist from HealthBridge Hospital. She drove all the way up from Orange County to spend a morning with us. It was perfect timing for Taylor to tell her that we are in fact planning to be at her wedding in March on Kauai. It was a goal for Taylor to do this, and she has never lost sight of that. Doctors are assuring her that she'll be cleared to fly on a plane by March, which is very exciting. A dear friend of mine from childhood is paying for us to go. Words cannot express my gratitude.

As you can imagine, it's been a busy two weeks. Taylor is working extremely hard, and every day we have some kind of therapy in addition to her full day at CNS, but no complaints from Taylor, even though we come home thoroughly exhausted. This week Taylor will be joining her classmates for a tai chi PE class offered on Mondays and Wednesdays. We will slowly start to integrate little things into her schedule so she can be at school until 12:35 in the afternoon both of those days. Taylor is over the moon, and this is the beginning of a giant step forward.

I don't speak often of the hard moments we're in, but they are always around (most of the time undeserving of energy or focus), and they are difficult. Sometimes unimaginable. The aftermath will be around for a while, and I will embrace it in order to remain focused and steady.

Journal Entry Day 189
November 26th, 2014

It is with enormous gratitude that I sit down to write one of my last journal entries to share with all of you. What a perfect time of year, as Thanksgiving has always been my favorite holiday. A celebration of thanks and giving with huge amounts of gratitude for everything we have been given. I have much to be thankful for this year, especially Taylor. She is alive and she will continue to be determined and focused on her own goals. Moments and days can be difficult, and it's hard for me to watch her struggle, but I know she will find her way. Somehow, she will do it. I am grateful she has accepted this challenging journey as part of her life.

Most of these last six months have been about embracing patience and acceptance. I still pause and attempt to inhale both of those things often. We're slowly settling into our new pace, and what our new life looks like. Taylor will hopefully continue to kick some serious ass. Her goals are still the same. My goal is to give her everything that she could possibly need to help her achieve them.

CHAPTER 14

Life

It was December, 2014. We were in a routine with Taylor and our schedules were working. Taylor had a busy schedule between her rehabilitation clinic, school, therapists, doctors, and a bit of downtime. The girls were around more during winter break, and it felt good. I always tend to miss my family in Colorado this time of year. I miss the snow, the change of season, and like clockwork, I tend to feel a little alone come the holidays.

It was Christmas Eve and I was on the phone talking to my sister, Lisa, who lives in Denver. She has been to visit several times since June and helped me enormously in wrapping my head around the business side of being Taylor's advocate. She was working for a hospital at the time and always had the best advice. Needless to say, Lisa and I are extremely close. On that phone call, Lisa proceeded to tell me that our mom had been diagnosed with stage four esophageal cancer.

What the hell? I didn't know how much more I could handle at that point. I might lose my mom? My mom had been twice to visit us since Taylor had been in the hospital. My biggest question was how the hell did all of that happen within a six-month time period? My poor mom was really sick. She had been so supportive of me, so helpful and loving. How would I help her while I was so deep in Taylor's world of recovery? I was heartbroken, and the thought of losing her then was devastating. Life, and the curve balls it throws...

119

Journal Entry Day 211
December 31st, 2014

As another year comes to an end, it's always an interesting time to reflect. I personally have reflected a lot in these last seven months, but on this eve of 2014 coming to an end, I feel it's appropriate for me to write in this journal for what possibly may be the last time. What a year it has been. A year of heartache, pain, and sadness. A year of letting go, and at the same time, accepting, embracing, and understanding. Many memories, weeks, and months of this year were spent letting Taylor show us the way. The results have been countless, but surrender and trust have been a gigantic part of the journey for me.

Starting on January 5th Taylor will be on her school campus every day. She will still attend CNS six hours a week for another year or two, but her school day will be designed especially for her, and she will take it from there. Many people will be watching very closely to make sure Taylor is given the opportunity to thrive at her own pace. It's an exciting but nerve-wracking transition ahead of her for me, and we want to set her up for success.

If I were granted wishes, my first would be for that rewind button. Since that doesn't exist, I wish for love to surround us always. I wish to be present in the moment and grateful for every single gift that comes my way. I also wish the same for all of you.

None of these last seven months have been easy, and without this whole village behind us, there are times when I think I could have broken into little pieces. When your world is turned upside down in a split second and your child is torn away from you and suffering, there is no other choice but to hold on tight and do the best you can. As I often say, this has been quite a year. It is a year I will reflect on sometimes with great sadness, but most of the time with a wealth of gratitude. My faith and hope have been tested but remain intact. I remain a firm believer in love because I know it is powerful beyond comprehension. I know it can turn the most painful and challenging of circumstances into something wonderful. Taylor has touched the hearts of many children and adults. We will all forever be changed by knowing her through this journey. I am proud to be her mom, and I am proud to be going through this journey with her, as hard as it is and as hard as it will be. I am lucky she is mine, and we are lucky to have all of you.

Good riddance 2014! I'm quite finished with you.

As I raise my cuppa tea, here's to a new beginning. A new year full of kindness, human compassion, and love. Most importantly, here's to a 2015 full of gratitude for what we are given, all new journeys good and bad, and the courage to accept them as they are.

Godspeed my dear friends and family, Godspeed.

● ● ●

I could go on and on about how fantastic my mom was, and she was determined to beat cancer. She was going to press on, fight it, and show up every day to do that. You can see where I get it from. My mom, Lollie, was awesome. One of the most delightful people to be around. The biggest take away for me as an adult is that she was compassionate, happy, and fun to be around. She had a wonderful sense of humor. She also raised five extremely strong-willed Italian/Irish women almost single-handedly. Need I say more?

My mom always remained positive and hopeful and she never let anyone rain on her parade. When I was on tour with Neil Diamond, my mom was the one who traveled with my kids so I could see them, and she did that six times. She always said yes, and would drop her life without hesitation. My mom always rallied, and I love that part of her.

Between my four sisters and me, my mom was known as 'Itsie' to her eleven grandchildren. Itsie started by taking the oldest one when he turned thirteen on a trip of his choice. This became a tradition, and to my mom it was something special to have with each one of them. Itsie had taken Taylor on her New York City Broadway trip the year before 'that day' happened, and it was great for both of them. It was that special bonding time that you never forget. Itsie had four more grandchildren to take on trips. Emma and her two cousins, who happen to be three weeks apart in age, and Charlie, the youngest nephew and grandchild. My mom was motivated and more determined to finish her trips with her grandchildren than anything, and her exact words were, "I wanna beat this damn thing."

She tried her damnedest. Itsie took Emma and her two cousins on an Alaskan cruise in June of 2015 only six months after her diagnosis. Charlie, my youngest nephew, never got his trip. My mom passed away in March of 2016—four days shy of her seventy-sixth birthday.

• • •

Taylor, Emma, and I went to say our goodbyes four days before my mom left this earth, and one of the most beautiful moments for me was watching Taylor hold her hand and sing to her while she lay in bed. My mom looked wistful. It was a few minutes I'll never forget as long as I live. My mom and daughter, who were so far apart in age but had both been through so much. The two bravest women I knew. They have both given me the gift of courage and clarity in my life because of the grace they have each shown me. My sweet mama. We all miss her.

CHAPTER 15

The Real Stuff

School wasn't easy for Taylor while she was also attending CNS for rehab. She was only on campus five hours a week and missing out on a lot of things. Taylor was feeling a disconnect from her peers. This obviously made her sad, but it served as motivation to work harder in order to get back to school full-time so she could graduate with them. "I'm going to walk across that stage with my class, and show them I can do it." Those were Taylor's exact words.

You go girl.

At the start of the school year in September of 2015, Taylor agreed to ease back into her real school. Come October she would go to tai chi class, choir, and stay for lunch. The headmaster and I had discussed this as being the only option to help her be successful in her re-entry. The last thing we wanted to do was set her up for failure. The idea of only those two classes didn't thrill Taylor at first, but the goal was to make her feel included. That piece she liked, and Taylor thrived by having a goal. Despite her really wanting to get back to schoolwork, Taylor was keenly aware of what she was not capable of doing. I know that was painful for her because it certainly was for me. Taylor would share stories about the lunch table being difficult. She wasn't able to follow conversations as quickly as she used to. There was one day when everyone got up and left her by herself at the table without saying goodbye, and she cried. I was devastated for her.

As far as the classroom, Taylor really couldn't go back to regular classes because she wouldn't be able to follow along. It wasn't possible for her, and Taylor was well aware of that. That led to us discussing a special school for her to attend a little later in the game. It would be one-on-one learning in order for her to catch up during summers between the school year. Taylor would later attend Fusion Academy, which is one teacher to one student, in addition to her school and CNS for three years. She was always working, and her dad and I were constantly driving her from one place to the other. The goal was for her to graduate in June of 2018 with her peers, get the credits she needed for a high school diploma, and walk across that stage.

Journal Entry One Year Later
June 4th, 2015

It is with sadness that I sit down and reflect on what this past year has brought. More importantly, what this past year has brought Taylor. A year ago today, saying goodbye to Taylor and Emma that morning as we parted, I had a moment with myself at the backdoor, feeling overwhelmed with emotion as another summer was only a week away. My feeling of not wanting to leave them was especially powerful and unusual. And here I sit one year later.

June 4th is a day I will always remember, and I'm quite sure that many of you feel the same way. I, in the challenging moments, chose to always see the growth and measure it against where we were the afternoon of June 4th last year. Those days were dark, hard, sad, exhausting, and so questionable. So much so, that they are difficult to look back on, hence my sadness.

We have all come a long way, and we have all learned how amazing it is to go through something like this. Our families and friendships and the strength of our community have all been put to the test beyond anyone's imagination. I still, and always will, feel deep and boundless gratitude towards all of you.

Taylor's life is different, and she is different, but every day she tackles this with an open heart and an open mind. I think what is most difficult these days is Taylor coming to terms with how different she is. She has slowly become more aware of what that difference means, and she is more understanding of the work that lies ahead. Taylor continues to work hard every single day, challenging that memory, doing her therapies without fail, and asking a lot of questions so she can be crystal clear on things.

She starts a new school next week in order to attend summer school and do some catch-up work. It's a one-on-one school in Pasadena called Fusion Academy, and Taylor is eager to get a fresh start somewhere.

Since the beginning of this year, we have done a lot to heal emotionally. One of those things was going to Fire Station 86 to say a big thank you to the men and women who first attended to Taylor and transported her to the hospital. I remember seeing some of them 'that day' in the hall, but there was nothing like seeing them next to Taylor with cupcakes in her hand. It was pretty fantastic and obviously emotional for all of us.

They told us that they don't get those kinds of visits often, and we had made their day. Dean, the paramedic who never left Taylor's side, was overwhelmed with joy to be able to shake her hand and later give her a squeeze goodbye. We took a chance on Dean being on duty, and of course, he was. We talked and shared details and a lot of emotions about 'that day.' It was a call that no firefighter or paramedic wants to receive, and they will never forget it.

Taylor and Dean climbed into the back of ambulance 86 where she asked him a lot of questions. We all listened, and a lot of us cried. Dean told us she stopped breathing three times, and he explained to Taylor how he helped her breathe each time to get her back. That was a lot to take in for me.

Dean is no rookie, and he looked straight at Taylor and said, "Well, Taylor, I know you have something amazing to go and do. I wonder what that will be."

Needless to say, we have some new friends at Fire Station 86.

I often find myself looking across the room at Taylor and Emma in awe of them both, and what they have been through this year. What they have seen, learned, and felt gives them a perspective on life that most people never get to have. I hope we continue to accept that perspective as one of the many gifts in this. Above all, Taylor is loving, kind, and not afraid to stand up for herself when she needs to. Her tenacity over the last year has truly floored me. And now more than ever, Taylor's bravery is inconceivable at times. I have learned that compassion and courage can get someone through a difficult period in their life, whatever way it looks on the other side. I have also learned that sometimes in life we could all use a fresh start. I hope that you will all join me in wishing Taylor a successful fresh start at this one-year mark, June 4th. This first year is behind us.

· · ·

This is where I kick myself. All of us were so focused on Taylor and her goal, that Emma was slipping. Emma mentioned to me last year that she wanted to stay with me when Taylor went to her Dad's house (and vice versa) so she could get a break. I knew she needed more attention and alone time with us, without Taylor always being a distraction away from her. I agreed it was a good idea, but with our work schedules and how we planned our weeks when we had the girls, she would be alone a lot. With that said, I tried for that first month to have sleepovers with her, dinners, go to movies, and spend time together with no one else around. It only happened a few times. Emma started to say no to every invitation I offered her, and I sensed a change in her right around that time.

It was in a teacher conference in the fall of her sophomore year when I heard Emma was ornery and not participating, and that her grade was slipping quickly. This was drama class where Emma usually excelled. I was extremely confused when I left that meeting because who gets a D in drama? For the next few weeks, I sought out other teachers, spoke to parents of her friends, and finally spoke to Emma.

She was hanging out with the wrong kids, pushing the envelope, and obviously screaming out for attention. That was an intense year for me with Emma. She was hanging on by a thread at this private school, which was a privilege to attend. At the risk of being expelled, her dad and I jumped into action by being open and brutally honest with her. The reality of Emma possibly having to leave that school spooked her, sparked some anger, and also made her lash out at us. I then hired a therapist/friend to come spend time in our house in order to help break this down the right way for at least Emma and me.

At the end of her sophomore year, Emma and I had some breakthrough days that were rough, but I'm so glad we had those. We eventually got to the bottom of it when Emma became willing to crack wide open. She was able to let her anger out at me and also show her sadness about my divorce from her dad. Then came the situation we were in and that damn day that changed us all. She felt lost, and she especially felt like we had all left her behind. Especially Taylor, her big sister, who had vanished.

Emma also needed to know that I was sorry. I was personally sorry for everything that she had to endure as an innocent child in all of this. I explained to her that I was sorry for divorcing her father, I was sorry that we lived in two houses, and I told her that I was especially sorry for what happened to Taylor because it happened to all of us. I told her I would never in my life be more sorry about anything. That was when the tears came flooding for both of us, and that was when I saw her change. Emma needed to see me feel it, and I had only done that in private or in my own therapy sessions because I wanted to protect my children from feeling *my* pain as well as their own. The magic happened when I was willing to share my vulnerability and humility with Emma, and that was the true game changer.

Through a lot of tears and a lot of pain for a couple of months, Emma and I came out on the other side. She also worked really hard at school to change things. I explained to her that I desperately wanted her to get her driver's license (and possibly a car), which could be her ticket to freedom—something her sister may never get. That was enticing to Emma since she'd wanted to drive a car since she was three years old. After that breakthrough, I paid close attention to Emma and made sure we had open conversations about what she needed. Her grades went up, especially in theater class where she found an outlet to express herself. She also got that driver's license and later came the Subaru. I have endless respect for Emma and the dig she did into herself through that hard time.

part
five

CHAPTER 16

Graduation

On June 14th, 2018, Taylor's class graduated from high school, and she joined them on that stage. Four years ago on June 4th, I wouldn't have believed anyone if they tried to tell me that would be happening exactly four years later. That would have been day ten in the hospital, and I couldn't have imagined this for Taylor. I was bursting at the seams with excitement. She wanted to borrow a blue dress of mine to wear on graduation day, and when she tried it on, I cried. I was overwhelmed with emotion. I had always hoped that graduation would happen for her, and I had constantly encouraged Taylor to believe it herself. Every single piece of hard work that she had put in was for that goal. Thursday, June 14th, 2018, was graduation day. Woot woot!

A couple months prior, Taylor had chosen to sing a song that I used to play repeatedly when Taylor was two years old. She would watch me get ready for work and would be in front of the mirror singing along with all her might, insisting that I play it over and over again. It was "I Hope You Dance" by LeeAnn Womack (if you haven't heard that song, you should take the time to have a listen), it always made Taylor smile as a munchkin. When she told me she would be singing it at graduation I'm quite sure I burst into tears again. Let's just say that in that month of June, I had shed enough tears of joy to cover a lifespan, and I was absolutely thrilled for Taylor.

Picture this: Taylor in her Taylor Blue dress sitting on a

stool and the stage lit a dim blue. Accompanying her was Nate, on guitar, and Ivan on upright bass. They had both visited us at HealthBridge and played music for Taylor before she could speak again. Her classmates were behind her in rows of chairs, and she had a microphone in hand. My breath was taken away. The audience roared and applauded her before she began. She said calmly, "Ivan and Nate came to visit me when I was in the hospital four summers ago to play music with me, and so it is truly an honor to be up *here* playing music with them." The applause continued while the music started.

Taylor brought the house down, and it was deeply emotional for a lot of us. Even her classmates were wiping away tears, and when she finished her song each row of her classmates began to stand up. Within ten seconds the whole theater was applauding in a standing ovation for her. Of course, we were in awe from our seats. My friend Nancy, my sister Lisa, and Emma were next to me. So happy, so emotional, and so incredibly proud of her.

Campus time had ended in May for the seniors because they start what was called 'senior projects' before graduation. They didn't really attend classes per se, but they worked on presenting their projects to faculty and staff at the beginning of June. Taylor had decided to do what I named a 'Taylor Talk,' but I had no idea what to expect. She had been chosen as the first presenter, and I was nervous *for* her. Taylor talked about 'that day,' getting hit by a car, and how it had changed her. She talked about brain injury and how difficult it is. She was in front of all her peers as a poised, beautiful, confident senior explaining to them how what had happened to her had completely changed her forever. Taylor shared her struggles and specifically her thoughts. She shared details regarding her therapies and what the past four years had looked like from her perspective. As she spoke, you could have heard a pin drop for eight minutes. She was passionate as she shared with them, explaining to her classmates for the first time how different she felt, not only in her body, but around her peers. Her project was about perseverance and patience along with persistence, and she was fascinating to watch. My thoughts during the applause were *good for her, and what a bold move right there.*

Journal Entry Four Years Later
June 4th, 2018

Dear Friends,

I know, it's been a while, hasn't it? Although, truthfully, being that it was four years ago is hard to believe. I've shaken my head a few times today in disbelief, especially when I was at school listening to Taylor speak in front of her peers during senior projects.

I have been encouraged by a few of you in the past few weeks to write a journal entry. I gave it some thought and here I am. I have missed writing to you all because not only has this been very cathartic for me, it has also been my way to stay in touch with you all for so long. Especially on my hardest days. The good news is, those hardest days are behind us. Taylor and I have seen some of you, but many of you haven't seen us, so why not do an update?

I sit in so much gratitude as I reflect back to 'that day' four years ago. So much gratitude that I'm bursting at the seams with pride, leaning into this bittersweet time that many of you are experiencing right along with me. Graduation, a time that certainly tugs at those heartstrings. A time that has sent me personally into an emotional, reflective, accepting, and grateful space.

We've come a long way, and Taylor especially has come a long way. No one, and I mean not one single person, doctor, or specialist four years ago could have told me that Taylor would be graduating from high school along with her peers. I would not have believed them, and I also don't think anyone knew it would be possible. Taylor has shown true resilience, tenacity, and downright grit, especially in these last two years. Taylor's character has been tested, and she has been physically challenged in ways that have left her feeling defeated. Yet she always, without fail, has picked herself up and started over with a smile on her face. Her indomitable spirit has rarely surprised me because if one thing has held steady, it's her spirit.

Honestly, I have been a giant (and I mean giant) pain in her butt, but I don't think she would have it any other way. Taylor will continue to do occupational, speech, and physical therapy throughout the summer, and she does it without a complaint. Ultimately, she knows I am not here to be her friend. I am her mom, and I am here to see her through this, however long that takes.

Taylor has had an enormous and beautiful community of people not only rooting for her, but also spending time with her, working with her, nurturing her spirit, and giving Taylor a piece of what they have. Warriors, all of them. All of you. The compassion that our community has shown to us has been something that I will remember forever. The feeling is indescribable, and yet I feel lucky to have been going through it with all of you by my side.

I stand strong in hindsight now, and even with a lot of work still ahead of me, hindsight is a beautiful thing. In my life, I hope I never go through something so difficult ever again. I have a better understanding now that good and bad things happen in life, and I have learned this from Taylor: how you respond to the bad things that happen is what makes you, *you*. That, my friends, sums up Taylor's journey through and through.

I hope you always keep a piece of this in your hearts and

never forget the strength and compassion you all showed us. I may have to push this journal aside, but please know that it has meant the world to me that you all have been a part of it. You have been here for the whole ride, and I always held hope that we would get where we are. Today, here she is, and here we are four years later. Wow!

CHAPTER 17

Coincidence

It was September of 2019, and I was having left knee issues for the first time in my life. I had been skiing, playing tennis, and working out regularly, and the pain was frustrating me. After finally seeing a sports medicine doctor and finding nothing wrong mechanically in an MRI, I was given a prescription for twelve sessions of physical therapy. I chose one near my home and let the referral note sit on my desk. I'm somewhat athletic and know my body well, so I decided on my own to not go to physical therapy but instead to push through it. I was still working out but stretching more and babying it when I did physical activity. It truthfully wasn't working and the nagging pain was still there.

In December I had my first ski day of the season and on the last run of the day I took a fall and tweaked my knee. The pain was different and pretty bad. So back to LA I went and made my first physical therapy appointment. I stalled for four more weeks, but finally got there. I have to admit I thought physical therapy would be somewhat lame and assumed I would probably learn nothing I didn't already know, but I was going to give it a whirl. I could resist no longer.

My first session was long, and I met several lovely women who worked there. One was the owner of the clinic, another was a massage therapist, and another went from patient to patient doing ultrasound therapy; her name was Diana. I went in with a goal in mind. I told them the details regarding

my knee, the injury, and the pause between getting my prescription and actually going to physical therapy. The exciting
part was I felt great walking out of there, like my knee had
been doctored up. It was encouraging to say the least, and
my mind had changed about what physical therapy would be
for me. I made my second appointment, which I changed two
times, and finally went on Wednesday, January 15th.

I did exercises and stretches with Kim, massage therapy
with Jackie, and then Diana came into the room to put the
ultrasound machine on my knee for ten minutes. We got to
chatting a little and she asked if I had kids, and I told her
about Taylor and Emma.

"My youngest is a senior graduating in May which is beyond exciting."

Diana asked where my kids went to school. I told her the
name of their school, and she said, after a long pause "...Oh
yeah, I know that school. It's right by my house."

We talked about the traffic on that street because of two
high schools being within four blocks of each other and how
crazy it was these days. Diana then said, "Did you hear about
the accident a while back when the three girls were hit by the
car coming down the ramp?"

I looked at her and said, "I sure did hear about that."

I let her continue to talk because I was thinking, *One of
the worst days of my life? You mean that one?* I let her finish, and then we sat in silence as I fought back tears thinking
about that damn day, which even people like Diana remember. The machine beeped and I switched positions.

"You wanna hear something crazy? One of those girls was
my daughter, and she spent sixty-six days in the hospital with
a traumatic brain injury."

I was looking at Diana, and I swear her face went completely white and her body froze. She put down the ultrasound.

"What? No way."

"Yes, my daughter and two of her friends."

Diana didn't move. She kept staring at me. Silence and more silence as she stared at me and her hands started to shake.

"Do you want to hear something even crazier?" she said.

I was thinking in my head, *You won't top that girl, but sure! Try me.*

She continued, "That was my stepdad who was driving that car."

I jolted up so I was able to see her eyes. I grabbed her hand, looked to the ceiling and back down again, and replied, "I can't believe this is happening right now."

Tears from both of us and we immediately got talking about how Taylor was doing, how her stepdad was coping, and some more details about 'that day.' Both of us were shocked that in a city that big, here we were.

Diana told me that her stepdad is the nicest man, and since that fateful day, his life had been difficult. The stress had caused his blood pressure to skyrocket, and he had had three strokes in the five years since the accident. He had gone blind in one eye and didn't go a day without thinking about what had happened, replaying it in his head. He was working on finding some peace with it, but it had been really difficult for him. I shook my head in disbelief as Diana went on. Some of what she was saying I had learned, and what I didn't know made me emotional. Things like: he wished he could erase 'that day,' he couldn't sleep at night, couldn't focus, and was haunted by what had happened.

I asked Diana to please get a message to him for me. I started to tell her about Taylor's first day in the hospital and what I felt toward the driver of the car. I told her I wasn't angry at him, that I had always, even from the moment I heard what happened, forgiven him. I had learned then that this man was

139

a father and a husband. I also knew that he had been at the scene, distraught and extremely upset. I had known nothing more about him at the time, but my gut feeling was right on, and I moved it all aside in order to focus on Taylor. I had always known the driver would have to go through his own journey, which certainly would not be an easy one. I learned that to be true after speaking to Diana about him. His life has also been different since 'that day,' which had brought on significant challenges, even for him and his family.

Diana asked to see a picture of Taylor, and I quickly grabbed my phone as I explained to her that Taylor was lucky to be alive. As hard as Taylor's recovery had been and the challenges she faced on a daily basis, she was able to walk, talk, and enjoy life. I briefly detailed the cognitive struggles that Taylor still faced, but for the most part I made it sound like Taylor was leading the life of a typical nineteen-year-old. Diana was thrilled to hear all of it, and I ended with, "There is something else you need to know. All of us involved would take 'that day' back if we could. Getting it back isn't possible, so on we go." I took a deep breath and continued, "My only hope is that he has come to find some peace in all the madness."

She agreed and said that's not how life works; you can't take it back.

"You're right, but what's happening here is also how life works, and I'm sitting in front of you, and you're sitting in front of me talking about this, and Diana, what a crazy coincidence." The timing of it all.

Diana and I hugged goodbye, and I walked into the elevator thinking about the driver—sending him love, but also getting emotional over the entire human connection that had happened in those thirty minutes. I was sure of one thing, meeting Diana that way and at that time, in the big scheme of things, was absolutely meant to be.

I had been going back to physical therapy two days a week and hadn't seen Diana since that interaction. Apparently she had gotten really sick that same week we first spoke—high fever and horrible stomach flu. I asked about her every time I went, and she didn't return to work until three weeks later on February 5th at the tail end of my therapy treatments. I was happy to see her after being able to give that interaction some time and thought. She was doing a therapeutic ultrasound on my knee. It was quiet and I wasted no time.

"Diana, did you get a chance to talk to your stepdad and tell him you met me?"

"Of course I did, and I told him face-to-face so I could see his reaction. He had a little smile while I was telling him that I met you. I told him 'Taylor's mom is lovely, and she wanted to send a message to you. She wanted you to know that she has never felt anger toward you. She didn't blame you, and she was asking about how you were.'"

Diana said he had tears and couldn't believe what a small world it is sometimes. He was happy to know that Taylor was doing well and wanted me to know that he had known her name since day one. He was also aware that she was the one most injured 'that day.' He had been praying for her ever since.

I asked Diana if she thought her stepdad would be willing to meet us someday. I told her how I think it would be good for all of us to get a chance to see one another and be in the same room together.

That's when my heart started to burst. I got emotional and realized that this could be our chance to bring this life-changing event full circle for Taylor, the driver, Emma, and me. To possibly heal our hearts and souls. Life, it's quite amazing sometimes.

CHAPTER 18

Full Circle

I was planning to move to Denver, Colorado after Emma graduated from high school in the summer of 2020. My plan was to get Taylor situated back at college, then I would move to Denver where my sister, Lisa, and brother-in-law, Ted, lived. I was single and felt a pull to get out of Los Angeles and closer to family. After my mom passed away, my other three sisters had opted out, so Lisa and I owned my mom's townhome together in Basalt. It wasn't always easy to get on a plane from Los Angeles, but moving to Denver would allow me to drive to the mountains on a whim, and be able to go home more often. I wanted a break from the big crowded city, but knew I could fly back to LA for work if needed. Mostly, I needed something different.

In June of 2019, I met with a realtor in Denver to start looking at homes for my move. I drove up to Basalt after that because I had decided to stay for the entire month of July. The mountain air and wide open space felt good to me. I invited the girls to join me for either a short stay or a long one and gave them the option to bring a friend with them if they wanted.

Mike and I were co-parenting very well at that point, and summers seemed to me more relaxed and not so routine. The girls each made a visit out, and the last five days of July I spent by myself before heading back to Los Angeles.

That's when I got a phone call from a friend of mine, who

I had known since middle school. Annie had come out of a yoga class, and told me she had the thought during the end of class that I should meet a certain John Fox. I did meet John, and within a couple of months after meeting him, my whole plan had changed, in a good way.

John lived in Aspen, Colorado, and although I wanted to move back home, it didn't pose a possibility for me while being a divorced mom. I was forty-eight years old and John turned fifty, three days after our first date. I'm sure you all remember that evil COVID happened in March of 2020, so our *meet-cute* timing was true perfection. John is my soulmate, the man I've always dreamed of being with. He is my champion and the greatest bonus dad to my children. I'll be thanking Annie for the rest of my life.

John and I were engaged fairly quickly, by December of 2020. Emma and I had moved to Colorado that August, after my house had sold and we had had ample time to say our goodbyes. From March to July of that year, things had not been easy. Their dad had gotten extremely ill and had been unable to see the girls for a good part of two months, which meant John had jumped in head first.

Emma, an angry senior, had started doing school from her bedroom. Taylor, in her best interest, had been home for that school year. She already had been doing her second year of college from home and online, so she had adjusted before any of us. What a time that was.

John had driven out to LA when the world shut down. During that time, it was the four of us in tight quarters in my then seventeen-hundred-square-foot house. Despite some really hot and hard days, we made the best of it. We didn't have a pool, but we had a hose. Honestly, after a couple of those days with Emma stomping through the house and us losing patience with one another, I thought to myself, *There is a chance John could get in his car one day and leave me.*

He didn't do that. He took a few necessary bike rides, but we all wound up learning how to get through it together in a unique way.

We now look back on those months as a special time. John got to know my kids, in good moods and bad, and they got to know him. Together we got creative with what to do, what to cook, and what to do the next day after that. The days were long and slow, but we all have fond memories of that time together.

Come June, Emma quasi-graduated from high school at a drive-in graduation. She missed out on her senior trip, senior prom, and those last two months of what being a senior is like. They all got jipped, but Emma managed to keep a good attitude and was truly excited about moving to Colorado at the end of the summer. Los Angeles was a hard place to be during that time, and we were all ready for a change.

Emma decided to take a gap year before starting college, and Taylor would head back to college in August. She was willing to follow all the strict COVID guidelines and was anxious to get back.

John went back to work in mid-June in Colorado while the girls and I took advantage of the couple of months we had left in Los Angeles. The last two months were difficult, yet wonderful. Goodbyes after so long are never easy.

• • •

Taylor and I discussed inviting the driver of the car over to our house before we moved. Diana was willing to help me coordinate a meet-up, and Taylor was finally open to it after all we'd been through. Six months after 'that day' when I asked Taylor if she would like to see the driver of the car, her response was, "Yeah, I'd like to see him! I'd like to see him BEHIND BARS!"

I was shocked at first, and then I remember understanding where she was coming from. It was all very black and white to her, and at that particular time he was the bad guy. Taylor saw the driver as the one who did that to her, the reason she couldn't remember the last two months, and why her life had forever changed. She wasn't ready to grasp the thought of him being a victim as well.

I would periodically check in with Taylor and where she stood with her feelings toward the driver, hoping for a change, and always anticipating that teaching moment. Many years later we would learn the driver of the car was not at fault. It then became easier for Taylor to let go of the blame, dig deep, and find some compassion for him. It took her six years to get to that place of forgiveness, and I let her have that time.

We arranged a day that worked for all of us. Diana and I knew it would be good for Taylor, the driver, and both of our families—a healing and an opportunity to come together. We were deep in COVID at this time, so we arranged to meet in my backyard. You had to walk down the driveway on the side of the house in order to get to the back patio. I heard them coming down the driveway, and I felt a wave of excitement, but also pure dread.

I couldn't believe what had happened to these two people. Lives had forever changed in the blink of an eye, and here we were, seconds away from meeting, face-to-face, this man, who has been in my thoughts every single day for the past six years.

His name was Tony. He was a tall yet soft-spoken, kind, and patient-looking man. Even though he was fifty-four years old at the time, he looked young and sweet.

Tony, his wife Mary, and Diana all stood in front of us as we introduced ourselves. Diana and I were immediately emotional. Taylor hugging Tony hello was one of the greatest moments to witness, and then they sat and chatted. Taylor and Tony spoke about how they were doing in detail, and it wasn't easy for either one of them to hear. Tony emotionally having to deal with what happened 'that day' and all that it did to him was heartbreaking.

Taylor, who doesn't remember a good part of two months, mostly spoke about the therapies she was still doing and some things that were still difficult for her. There was complete silence, and then Tony said to her "...well Taylor, you are such a beautiful young woman, and I'm so sorry that this happened to you."

"I'm so sorry this happened to you too," she said back.

Then the tears came flooding from Mary, Diana, and me as the two of them held hands. What a beautiful moment.

Taylor and Tony spent more time talking and we learned more about what the past six years had looked like for him and his family. It had not been easy for him, and Taylor showed great empathy listening to him speak. Taylor shared some things as well—mostly about school and the challenges, her friends and those challenges—as he was also deeply engaged with her. The rest of us listened intently.

Tony then asked Mary for the gift that he had brought for Taylor. Taylor was obviously touched and asked if she could open it. Tony had given her a beautiful leather-bound journal and a set of beads that had belonged to his mother, who had since passed away. He told Taylor that those beads bring good luck and good health, and they remain precious in their Lebanese culture. Taylor loved the gifts, and she was moved by his kindness. We said our goodbyes soon after that. All of us were grateful that that coming together happened. It changed me, and I'm quite sure it did the same for them.

The next day Taylor wrote Tony a thank you note:

8/12/20

Dear Tony,

Thank you so much for the incredible journal and beautiful beads. I feel more sad that this happened to you than me because you are one of the kindest and gentlest souls I've ever known.

Take care of yourself, and I hope we meet again in the future.

Sending love eternally,
Taylor

• • •

The move to Colorado came next, and John and I were married by Annie in October of 2021. We lived in what was my mom's home for over a year while we built one two blocks away. Life had certainly come full circle for me.

part
six

CHAPTER 19

Nowadays

Despite her brain injury, her losses, and the residual effects that Taylor has to deal with, she has remained kind. In my opinion, you can get a long way in this world by being a compassionate human being. Her goals consist of having a career, driving a car, and maybe even raising a family someday. Time will tell. I certainly want all of that to happen for her. I also hope she continues to prove anyone wrong who has set limitations on her, or any traumatic brain injury survivor.

Taylor graduated from Linfield University in May of 2023, which I thought was next to impossible. I didn't think going *away* to college would be possible for her, let alone graduating from high school with a hefty scholarship in hand to Linfield University in little McMinnville, Oregon. Linfield was beautiful *to* Taylor and *for* Taylor. It was the perfect size university for her to get to know her way around, meet people, and even experience the roommate thing, which she definitely did. Most of the time it was great, and one time it was really bad. The professors and even the president of the school were wonderful to Taylor in every way. She was sad to say goodbye when that time came.

I heard the President of Linfield University, Miles Davis, speak when we first moved Taylor in for freshman year, and I told her she needed to go introduce herself at some point. One thing about Taylor, she has no fear about that sort of thing. Taylor, and Mr. Davis became fast friends after she walked into his office one day to make an appointment with him to introduce herself. He still, to this day, checks in with her and they meet for a meal once in a while when they are in the same city. They also share a love for basketball and he *still* lets her bend his ear. Linfield University was a nurturing prosthetic environment for Taylor in a way that I can't really explain. I only wish she could have stayed there forever.

Taylor's everyday world is better off being as simple as possible. If there is too much scheduled or too much to do, it can get complicated and extremely stressful for her. Stress, more than anything, causes her brain function to rapidly decline. Some things are hard for her to deal with, but she's learning what she can and can't handle.

Taylor lives in an apartment building that has a front desk, and everything else she needs is a quick ride up or down the elevator. Living alone is best for her in order to keep things tidy; there's no clutter, and things stay where she leaves them. In living alone, she has rules on using the stove, oven, or anything else that can be left on, in order to not make a mistake like putting a plastic cutting board in the hot oven for twenty-five minutes. Yes, that really happened, and it was bright green.

Taylor loves anything basketball, especially the Denver Nuggets, and anything musical theater or on Broadway. She can talk your ear off and is well-versed in all of it, but she can literally talk your ear off. It's all still a work in progress. She's learning how to tell a story without telling too many unnecessary details or totally losing the point of her story. Poof! Just like that, it can be gone. She's learning how to *follow* someone telling a story without things getting too boggled up, which still happens sometimes as well. Taylor is working on not getting lost in her surroundings, like being in someone's house and losing her way, or having a general sense of the direction from which she came. We're working on all of it.

I imagine her as a six-year-old a lot of the time, and that six-year-old needs help doing it, time to learn it, and then needs repetition upon more repetition until it sinks in. The key is doing it enough times for it to soak into the brain and stay there. She has shown massive improvement in many things because of redundancy. Multi-tasking and planning things out, still prove to be a challenge, but she is determined to manage those things someday.

A traumatic brain injury is rough to bounce back from. The good news is the brain is the only plastic organ in our human bodies willing to bend, and Taylor is living proof of that. Sometimes it's easy to get 'Taylor tired,' and that's what happens to me. It happens to other people, but I speak openly and honestly to her about how and why she is tiring. Taylor has a lot of friends, but I'm not sure what a relationship that truly matters will look like someday. I sure hope that will be in her future. Again, all a work in progress.

Rain Man still shows up once in a while with things like injuries or things that are important to her. That certain *thing* will stay on her mind, and she can't get her brain to stop obsessing over it, talking about it, and then talking about it some more. She's figuring out what makes people stay with her, and what makes people want to exit. Dory only visits once in a while, usually before Taylor takes her medication or when her brain and body are fatigued in the evening. No more drunk girlfriend; she's sometimes forgetful and repetitive, but so am I.

Taylor wakes up every day, and for that I am extremely grateful. She is genuinely content and happy even after all that's happened to her, and that means the world to me. Taylor has vowed to not touch drugs or alcohol. She has learned a lot from the nine neurologists she has met throughout this journey of hers, and they have all said the same thing to her: either drugs or alcohol could wind up being detrimental to her well-being. She has taken that advice very seriously throughout the years, and that is a big, giant monster that I hope stays in its place.

Taylor works out every single day because she knows cardio exercise improves her mental agility. She writes in a one-sentence gratitude journal every night before bed, and she continues to show up every single day for this thing called life. What more could I ask for?

For those of you who have experienced grief, you know that it never goes away. I will always grieve who Taylor used to be. I will also grieve those first fourteen years we had together. I remember her fondly and I always will. However, I am grateful for the Taylor I have now, and I am positive she is who she is today because of who she *was* at fourteen: the base brain she had going into this; her social skills along with her athletic and musical abilities. Those things all played an important role in her recovery, and who she will ultimately become.

Taylor survived that damn day and so did I. We come out different people no matter who takes the hit. I am well aware that Taylor could have died 'that day,' and I also could have had a heart-wrenching decision to make, which was discussed more than once. If she hadn't started breathing on her own, sitting up, or eating, there may have been no bringing her home at all.

In the world of Taylor, days are difficult sometimes. She gets sick in cars and airplanes easily, but most of the time she's prepared, because she's used to it happening now. Her body temperature gauge is wacky, which means she has a hard time in warm climates and rarely needs a jacket in cold ones. Short-term memory is still a struggle, but every six months I notice improvement. More important than all of that, Taylor chooses to live the best life she can.

When you're that close to dying, I'm quite sure you wake

up with a different appreciation for life. I believe we can all learn a little something from that, and maybe that will be her gift to share with the world.

"So be sure when you step. Step with care and great tact and remember that Life's a Great Balancing Act."
Oh, the Places You'll Go!
Dr. Suess

CHAPTER 20

My Takeaways

When I first sat down to write about what happened to me, I would repeatedly ask myself a few questions, mainly this one: what do I have to give to someone? My answer is this: I know that life as we know it can change on a dime. I know that you can be close to losing your child and feel totally and completely helpless, but in that feeling, you can learn to surrender completely. With that surrender came clarity, focus, and bravery that I never thought I had inside me. It's only from where I sit now, looking back in hindsight, that I know where it came from. It manifested when I was finally willing to let go, listen, and accept.

When I was willing to be open and accepting of what was going to happen.

Willing to understand that I didn't know the plan, and showing up every day had to be enough.

Willing to be courageous and trust my instincts.

Willing to fight in a respectful manner to be my daughter's advocate.

While I was learning, I would graciously challenge, question, and have conversations about what I knew would be best for Taylor. Normally I would have done what everyone said to do, but instead I trusted my gut and didn't settle for anything less. My hope is that if you're ever in a similar situation as me, that you will do the same.

The power of love also became very clear to me, and it

was almost palpable when I was with Taylor in those sixty-six long and difficult hospital days. I was willing to embrace the community that I thought I didn't have. I learned to rely on my family and friends, take it in, and receive everything that was being given to me. I was willing to accept the good things right along with the bad, and the bad far outweighed the good in those first couple of months.

Receive it was one of the many post-it notes I had stuck to my bathroom mirror soon after June 4th, and when I started to truly receive it all and let it in was when I became as vulnerable as I could possibly be. I knew that my only choice was to let go and let it all happen. I learned to lean in and trust. I began to trust in the divine timing of things, and I especially learned to trust myself and the bond between me and my firstborn child. I surrendered. That surrender, that knowing, and that trust didn't come easily to me, and don't think for one second I didn't try to fight it. I definitely did. It felt hard and extremely uncomfortable at times because I wanted to know the outcome. I desperately wanted to know the end result. When I stopped pushing against the surrender I finally received the biggest gift, possibly the only gift trauma can give you: I was peaceful and sure in all that was happening around me and in everything I was doing. That meant whatever the outcome was going to be was what it was going to be. I slowly found comfort in that.

After 'that day' I could have easily popped a Xanax on a consistent basis or become the alcoholic I've joked about becoming. I don't mean to be rude in joking about it for those of you who struggle or have struggled with addiction. For me, I hated the way Xanax made me feel, and I've rarely had more than one cocktail on any occasion. I joke because I wanted to find something to take away the pain.

Instead, I got in a boxing ring and I punched someone. I was on the tennis court whacking balls as hard as I could, and then I would go to yoga to find my center. For a few months I would seek out thirty-minute massages near CNS on a daily basis because being touched seemed to calm me. A lot of times at home, in the shower mostly, I would fall to my knees and completely fall apart, releasing it instead of holding it in. It was painful and exhausting, but I knew that I had to work through it. I learned and now know that there is no breaking through unless you break down first. Yes, that wonderful old saying.

I was seeing a therapist for a while, but there was only so much talking about the same feelings over and over I could do. For me it was about time. Time to heal and time separating us from that horrible day. Taking that time to actually grieve and feel things to my core. I think therapy is great when you have the right person, but so much of dealing with trauma and grief is letting it settle inside you, feeling it, which sucks, and then letting it out, which can also suck. I felt lighter, as if a weight was slowly lifting off of me, by letting it move through me. It still comes back to me, and it has not disappeared, but it feels different and manageable now.

Simply put, I will always miss who Taylor used to be. I'm still grieving that fourteen-year-old girl I said goodbye to that morning on June 4th, 2014. It is still difficult for me to see pictures or watch live videos of her before 'that day.' It's hard for me to see young women her age that she grew up with, and it's difficult for me to hear what they have and are accomplishing in life. I'm still dealing with that inside myself.

Taylor lost out on so many things during her high school career, and she had a promising future ahead of her for many reasons. She can't get those high school years back, but I have come to understand that a promising future is still ahead of her. That future that *used to be* just happens to look a little different, and I think Taylor's amazing book might be written twenty years from now.

In my many stages, waves, and different cycles of grief, came acceptance. I see who Taylor is and I consider it a gift to be able to watch and support her in finding her way in this world. Being able to embrace Taylor now and who she has become has been a huge part of my own journey. I hope it's obvious to you that she has astounded me. I feel lucky to be her mom and it has made this *hard paddle forward* completely worth it. After all, the outcome could have been very different for her, and I am positive that Taylor is *right* where she is supposed to be. For me, well, that is the silver lining in all of this. I often think that I would not be where I am today if 'that day' didn't happen. Strangely, I am hyper-aware that I am also here, exactly where *I'm* meant to be.

We met Tony. He and Taylor were able to show compassion to one another—my daughter who was hit and the man driving the car 'that day.' The day that turned all of our worlds upside down. It was a beautiful life lesson that came to my daughters early in life, which I see as a gift. It was a priceless moment between two humans that I will take to my grave as one of the best. Love conquered, and we could use a little more of that on this planet. I am thankful that both Taylor and Emma have chosen to accept what was given to them and what they found: resilience after feeling their anger, then the bravery they conjured after experiencing heavy sadness and fear.

It's not necessarily about being a positive person, even though I know that helped me. It was more about being willing to see the reason to hang in there, even on the worst days, and sometimes grueling hours, that were brutal. If you're on the floor in tears, stay there. Take time to break down, then shake it off, dust yourself off, and be willing to brave the way.

For me, it was being open to the challenge when you think a hospital may not be doing the right thing. Having the conversation about doing something differently than they might be used to—with teachers, headmasters, nurses, doctors, hospitals, rehabilitation clinics, and insurance companies. Be brave enough to ask for the best room in the hospital because the person you're advocating for, simply needs it. However you can, find your courage and be brave.

● ● ●

Is there a purpose in all of this happening? Not necessarily, but I believe that we all *choose* our own purpose in any given situation. I *chose* to be the warrior that I was, not because I knew I could, but because I wanted to.

Sometimes purpose can't always be seen without perspective, and to receive perspective requires patience and a lot of time. Honestly, I have only begun to understand that concept. Knowing that I need to give myself time, and Taylor needs to give herself time, has been a gift.

On the evening of June 4th, 2014, I only knew that I had to wake up every day and be helpful, hopeful, positive, and extremely thoughtful in my actions. I had to carry the weight while learning how to navigate through it one day at a time. I also knew my child was on the brink of death from getting hit by a car, and the world felt like it was whizzing by me, leaving us behind, especially me. I didn't like that feeling, and it put a hot, flaming fire inside of me.

My focus as you know was on Taylor and her recovery, which wound up guiding and defining me for a solid five years. It does not define me anymore, and little did I know that I would personally take a roller coaster of a journey deep inside myself *because* of 'that day' happening. Hindsight is a beautiful thing; it gives us the chance to step back and truly take nothing for granted. In my case, I like to refer to it as the collateral beauty that finally appeared after feeling and experiencing every piece of the collateral damage.

. . .

I wrote this last chapter during a week when Taylor was visiting us in Basalt. She doesn't come often, but some family things were happening and she wanted to be with us. On the last day of her visit, she was in the shower singing at the top of her lungs, disrupting the entire household. I put my face in my hands, took a deep breath, and thought for a moment. *Life. Go figure...*

In Reflection (some 10 years later)

Growing up, I always had a love for cars. I think it started with my dad, the car dealer who was always bringing home the cool, new, fast, and updated models. To this day, I really appreciate a nice car, and I love getting into the driver's seat of a beautifully designed vehicle. How ironic that a car hit my daughter and changed my life forever.

• • •

In reflection almost ten years since 'that day,' the transformation that I experienced through Taylor's own journey often has me mystified with wonder. I had decided to move out of Los Angeles before 'that day' happened because I was feeling alone. I had my kids and a handful of great friends, but ultimately I wasn't finding a partner or a future husband, and nothing felt like it had much meaning to me. The job I was in felt monotonous, and the routine of Taylor and Emma was going to shift eventually in only a matter of time. The odds of me being alone felt extremely high. I was craving more connection, more community, more meaning, and certainly love. Perhaps love from a man, mostly, but also love and acceptance. A feeling that I mattered to the world.

Boom! It happens. I am sitting on a hospital room floor when it hits me that I am the most important person in this scenario and I will certainly matter. I might be alone, but I will matter. The situation Taylor was in felt completely surreal to me. The one thing I was certain of was that I was her mother, she grew inside of me, and that was *everything* at that moment. I have known since the day she was born what Taylor needed, and I would have to go back to that knowing, that intuition, and that bond in order to save her life.

Little did I know that my village, my countless friends and family, would show up every single day to help me. They were a constant reminder that I was in fact not alone at all. The truth is I was never alone, and once I could be receptive to that love and support, it all changed. I was open to being hopeful, strong, and appreciative, and teaching myself to find the beauty in every small moment: in a hug, in a knock at the door, in laughter, or a good conversation that would make me cry. I was feeling everything to my core. I found the kindness and compassion in this world that I needed because every single person around me showed it. It fell right into my lap, and I started to believe that I was worthy of it. I began to believe that someday a man would truly love me for who I was. I have some large and heavy baggage in tow, but I embrace it and claim it as a part of me.

I taught myself to pause. I forced myself to sit in the quiet and the stillness of myself and sink into that. It didn't always feel good, but if you sit and are still long enough, you start to unravel in it. There is something to be said about that unraveling because <u>then</u> I was able to be the badass of a woman and mom that I was. I knew myself on a deeper level, and I started to listen more than I would talk.

I started to be more thoughtful before I took action. I took more in. I found strength and courage that sometimes shocked me. I also was able to embrace my own self and know that deep down inside my soul, I was not only a good person, but I was a fighter and an advocate in every sense of the word. *That* my friends, that right there became my greatest strength and weapon along the way: stepping out of my own way to understand everything about myself. I could truly see myself, and that was the superpower I needed.

I have an appreciation for the little things now. I have a

special gratitude for tiny and beautiful things that happen. I am especially empathetic to people who know trauma. I appreciate progress, people making themselves better humans, and I mostly appreciate people who rise to the occasion when life is hard. Babies and children warm my heart. I've always felt a connection to our little humans, but now I am extremely fascinated with them: how they learn, what they soak in, and what they have to say. Their wonderful little brains. It's all extraordinary to me, perhaps because Taylor had to start over at fourteen years old.

I was always drawn to parents of children with disabilities, but now I carry an understanding that is different. I was always patient with them, but now it's a different *kind* of patience.

My perspective and my goals in life have shifted. My relationships have flourished and multiplied. My perspective and clarity on the person I have become and want to still be is simply different. Therefore, all of this has in fact changed my life. Is it better? Definitely. Am I still evolving as a human being? Definitely.

What I learned most is this: I experienced great love and acceptance when I needed it the most, and because of that, I have a deep appreciation for people who help *other* people. Human compassion and understanding are precious and irreplaceable. I believe it is a magic potion for those of us who live on this earth together. It is my greatest hope that we can all seek that potion, and find strength in loving one another. I know I did.

*"Be bold—and mighty forces
will come to your aid."*
Goethe

ACKNOWLEDGMENTS

To my supportive writing team:
Anne Kurashige my first coach, Brad Swift my final coach, and
Alyssa Ohnmacht and Olivia Savard at Light of the Moon,
Inc. for holding my hand through this. You all took part in
lighting the fire I needed. Thank you. My editor Hanna, you
fit like a glove, and I so appreciate who you are. Milo Hudson, your polishing skills are marvelous, and I'm thrilled you
were a part of this.

Dr. Robert McDermott, I am honored to have you in my life.

Thank you to every paramedic, ambulance driver, first responder, social worker, nurse, therapist, doctor, and surgeon who we met along the way—Team Taylor. I am forever
indebted to you.

To our school community and every administrator, student,
and parent who touched our lives. We'll always remember.

Mike, thank you for being the father that you are to our children and never doubting my mama bear instinct.

Monica Wyatt and Mark Horowitz, you never said no, and you
never stopped giving and helping. Thank you for being my
friends.

Frances Pennington and Curt Smith, thank you for jumping
in and saying yes—always. Through my tears and fears, you
were there, and I won't forget.

Lauren Roedy Vaughn for being so instrumental in the success of Taylor. It is immeasurable and we love you.

Arash and Danielle, I am eternally grateful for you.

To my *sistas* whom I adore:
Marcelle Rowihab, Claire Hartley, Oonagh Gottlieb, Florie Bunzel, Maggie Rocker, Tanya Simpson Miller, Aubrey Thorne Carey, Ada Gorn, Jessica LaRocca, Sandy Campanella, Annie Cassidy, and Jen Gwartz. Thank you for being in this life with me.

Katie (my skin'n'blista) and Neil Diamond, you were always there. To my entire Diamondville family, thank you for wrapping your arms around us. You're the best second family a girl could ask for.

Dave Hillard and Kent Brugger, thank you for swooping in and having my back. That was no small task.

Nancy and Steve Carell, I will forever be amazed by your family. Thank you for your friendship, for loving and protecting me, and reminding me every day to laugh.

To my blood sisters:
Staci, Lisa, Jenny, and Mita. I love you bitches. Thank you for having my back no matter what that looks like.

To my precious mom, who is smiling down on us. My muse. Without her, I would not have been able to do what I did. Not a day goes by that I don't thank her for showing me how strong women can be, even when I was going it alone. Mama, thank you for teaching me what grace and humility look like. The girls and I miss you every single day.

. . .

John Fox, thank you for loving me and my daughters the way you do. Thank you for embracing our past and loving us more for it. You are the *only* one who could walk through this writing process with me because it takes an exceptional man. We hit the jackpot together the day we met. You are, and always will be, my reason.

My sweet Emma, thank you for being you. You were my comfort in this, and you survived this journey of yours with flying colors. Every day I learn from your hunger for adventure and your steadiness when life demands it.
I love you to tiny little pieces.

To my Taylor Girl, as tough as it is—you are still fighting the fight. Thank you for always remembering your manners, allowing people to help you, and *always* leading with your heart of gold. Without fail, you trust in love and kindness. You remain patient, steadfast, and tenacious as hell!
If only we could all be as brave as you.
I can't wait to see what you do with your magic.
I hope someday you can measure how much I love you.
Life awaits you; go and get it, girl.

. . .

To those of you that showed up tirelessly and gave,
you know who you are. Thank you for believing in me.
That belief not only made me believe in myself,
it carried me through this journey, as it still does.

ABOUT THE AUTHOR

Laurel lives in colorful Colorado with her husband, John. She works as a voice-over actor and can be heard in many popular television shows such as *Lethal Weapon*, *Angie Tribeca*, and *Manifest*, to name a few. Laurel enjoys being a substitute teacher for the public and private elementary schools in the Roaring Fork Valley. She also sings in a local band, and dabbles on the theater stage whenever she can.

LaurelCFox@gmail.com